KEEP IT BETWEEN THE LINES

A Family Guide to Keeping Youth Sports in Perspective

Petronio Morillo

Advice From A Friend Publishing

Contact the author at petroniomorillo.com

ISBN: 979-8-218-88180-1 (paperback),
        979-8-9941643-9-6 (ebook)
Copyright © 2025 Petronio Morillo
All rights reserved.

Advice From A Friend Publishing
Gaithersburg, MD

Praise for *Keep it Between the Lines*

"*Keep It Between the Lines* is more than a book about youth sports — it's a mirror for every parent, coach, and leader who cares about kids. Petronio captures the heart of what truly matters: joy, growth, and perspective. Every academy, every sideline, and every family needs this message."

— Alan Lydiate
Maryland State Youth Soccer
Association, Former Director

"Every season, I get the privilege to meet hundreds of wonderful soccer parents who truly want the best for their kids but get caught up in the competition and pressure to win or be the best. This book helps them step back and see things clearly, offering a different perspective. *Keep It Between the Lines* is honest, timely, compassionate, and real—it reminds us that youth sports are for the children, and that they should build confidence and joy, not anxiety. I wish every parent could read this before submerging themselves into youth sports of any level."

— Steve Knapman
Brit-Am Soccer Academy,
Founder

This book is dedicated to my sister. Jennie, you are my inspiration. Thank you for always being there for me, even when I couldn't see you. Thank you for my life and our Joy.

To the moon and back again, Sis.

Table of Contents

Forward

How I wish I had this book when my son started playing sports. *Keep it Between the Lines* cuts through the noise created by a system that fosters unending expectations and false hopes. Using clear guidance and real-life examples, Petronio reminds us that, as parents, we have the power to shape our children's experiences in youth sports. It calls on us to remember that the goal of youth sports is not to win but rather to support our children in being the best versions of themselves.

My family has known Petronio Morillo "Coach Pete" for much of my son's soccer career, first as an assistant coach, then as a head coach, and most recently as a private trainer. My son describes Coach Pete as firm but fair, a perfectionist who has high standards and the unique ability to care for every player equally. He makes soccer fun and creates a culture where mistakes are allowed, freeing players to be creative and to push themselves. For these reasons, my son considers Coach Pete to be his most important coach. For me, it is Coach Pete's talent, his deep knowledge of youth sports, and his vast experience coaching boys and girls that make him uniquely qualified to write this book.

While my family's journey into youth sports is unique to us, the themes are universal. Our son started playing soccer at age six in the local rec league, and we quickly realized he had a natural ability and passion for the sport. At age eight, he made his first travel club soccer team, and since then, our lives have revolved around soccer—practices, games, tournaments, private coaching sessions, and summer camps. Weekend and vacation plans were scheduled around games and tournaments. We shifted work schedules around practice times, organized carpools, and transported teammates. We spent thousands of dollars on club and tournament fees, private coaching, uniforms, video streaming services, team trips, and endless cleats and soccer balls. In return, my son's sports journey has given my family enormous joy and satisfaction as we have watched him grow as an athlete, teammate, and person. We have priceless memories and the satisfaction of watching our child develop his passion. We are grateful to have shared our experiences with the other families on my child's teams. We were a community, bound by our children's love of soccer and our love for our children.

Being a sports family is all-consuming.

If your child plays a club sport, you are likely taking them to practice several times a week, games once a week, and a weekend tournament every few months. Your child will probably be cross-training or engaged in other sports during the off-season. High school sports layered on top of club sports can mean your child spends upwards of twenty hours a week in athletics. When not playing their sport, there is a good chance they are working out, talking about sports, watching sports, or playing sports-related video games. They might even be strategizing about their future in sports.

And yet, despite the all-encompassing nature of youth sports, I found there is little guidance for parents. Looking back, information on how to approach my child's athletic journey mostly came from: (1) league rules, including the parent code of conduct, (2) the coach's rules, which typically focused on getting parents to refrain from telling them how to do their job, payment and attendance requirements, (3) recruiters and athletic programs whose main goal was to sell a product or service, (4) YouTube and other social media sites that generally focused on improving performance, and (5) other parents, either via conversations or discussions on parenting listservs. The information was often fragmented, unreliable, and not geared toward my specific situation or concerns. It made it easy to worry about what Coach Pete describes as "all the wrong things." Instead of focusing on the values that athletic competition teaches, we worried about team rankings. Rather than enjoying the moment, we were concerned about being good enough to play in college. Despite strong bonds with his teammates, we wondered whether our son should try out for a "better" team, especially since many of the strongest players moved on to more "prestigious" teams each year. Hearing about other teams participating in more out-of-state tournaments, traveling to Europe, or attending college showcase tournaments left us with the sense that what we were doing was never enough.

Somewhere during his junior year, I noticed a shift in my son's relationship to sports. His friends began dropping out of soccer, and he started focusing more on other academic and social activities. His focus on college shifted from the dream of playing soccer to the opportunity to explore new interests. Ironically, I credit much of that to youth sports. As Coach Pete notes in this book, the intangible skills taught by youth sports—confidence, camaraderie, resilience, and the desire to improve and expand oneself—extend beyond the field and are evident in how he is choosing to transition into the next phase of life

I encourage every parent, no matter your child's age or where you are in your sports journey, to read this book. This book will help tether you and your family to what is important, helping you stay focused and centered on your family's goals rather than subjecting you and your child to the unrelenting expectations rampant throughout youth sports. The shift in mindset outlined by Coach Pete can help you avoid the fear and anxiety inherent in our youth sports system and have a profound impact on your relationship with your child, well beyond athletics. Youth sports should be a time for your family to make special memories and form lasting friendships. Much of it still is, but I suspect many of us can remember when we, or a parent we personally witnessed, lost our bearings and behaved poorly or said something that hurt a child, either on the field or on the drive home. As Coach Pete says, let's take back youth sports and re-center the reason we got into them in the first place—for our children.

Sangita Chari
December 5, 2025

Introduction

After thirty years of working in youth sports, I've learned that sports can have a profoundly positive impact on a child's confidence, growth, and happiness. Sadly, that magic is fading as more and more parents bring pressure, criticism, and unrealistic expectations into what should be a joyful experience. I coached youth soccer professionally, leading boys' and girls' teams at the highest levels of competition. I managed indoor sports complexes in Maryland, Virginia, Pennsylvania, and New Jersey for twenty years, overseeing thousands of youth leagues across various sports. During that time, I developed a soccer-based child development program that has helped tens of thousands of kids over the past two decades. Working with children as young as eighteen months, as well as coaching championship matches in front of college scouts, has given me a unique perspective on the sports world. Coaches feel immense pride and joy watching their players have fun, play, and learn. It is a rewarding job, but it also presents serious challenges. The pressure placed on players and coaches is overwhelming.

In fact, I discovered that the more my teams won, the higher the expectations became—until they became impossible to satisfy. Over the years, I have witnessed the gradual decline in the joy of youth sports under the weight of misplaced priorities, overinvestment, and unrealistic expectations.

Sports offer numerous physical benefits for kids, including improved fitness, increased strength, greater endurance, better cardiovascular health, stronger coordination, and enhanced overall physical well-being. The social benefits can even be greater. Children learn to relate to their peers and form friendships. They communicate in groups, resolve conflicts with others, and collaborate in teams. In addition, the mental and emotional components of sports can be invaluable. Kids learn to manage their emotions as they tackle challenges, sometimes winning and sometimes losing. Sports demand discipline and commitment. Players will encounter and overcome adversity, unfair outcomes, and unsportsmanlike conduct. There is no doubt that youth sports are an important vehicle for teaching kids valuable life lessons.

The sports environment is an excellent way to teach kids about important issues such as commitment, hard work, losing, competing, and teamwork. While we should teach our children proper behavior, that isn't always what happens on ball fields and in gyms around the world. We've all seen the outrageous parents who yell at referees, other parents, and even their own children. I have often seen parents lacking any accountability for their behavior on the sideline, yet asking more of their kids on the field. Parents who lose control and distract attention from the game set a poor example. That's not what anyone wants in youth sports.

I have not been immune to the culture of adult bad behavior. When I started coaching, I believed that we had to win so my players could be noticed and recruited by colleges. Once they secured a soccer scholarship, the investment would truly pay off. I pushed my players to compete so we could climb the rankings and qualify for college showcase tournaments for the best national exposure. Through the process, I learned the truth about youth sports. The true purpose of sports isn't to create players who can play in college or pro; it's to bring people together. What matters most isn't the scoreboard or record books, but the fun kids have running around with friends. If you are considering starting youth sports for reasons other than fun, friendship, and fitness, you should reconsider.

I retired from coaching because I became disillusioned with the youth sports industry. I loved working with kids and watching them develop into excellent players, but I grew tired of seeing them hurt by adults' behavior, primarily parents. I don't believe sports parents ever set out to harm their children. The vast majority of parents on the sidelines are good people who want to raise good kids, but youth sports can be highly charged emotional events, and adults can become caught up and act in ways that contradict their own beliefs. I hope that most adults regret any harmful behavior, but that's not enough. We must work to put a stop to it. I'm sharing my ideas and experiences to help parents prepare for what's ahead. If we are aware, we can avoid some of the outrageous and hurtful behavior I've seen over the years and ensure our players have the best possible experience. I left coaching with a heavy heart, having witnessed the sport I love and the kids who play it being hurt repeatedly. I wrote this to help parents protect their families in the youth sports environment.

The focus of youth sports should remain between the lines on the field. These games and matches are about the children playing on the field—they deserve the spotlight. The focus should stay on them, not on parents or spectators. While competition brings pressure, mistakes, triumphs, and setbacks, parents don't need to add more stress from outside the lines.

Always remember that, as the parent, you are the ultimate decision-maker. You cannot pass this responsibility on to a coach or league official. Your number one priority as a parent is to ensure no harm comes to your child. No coach, league, or sport should ever take precedence over that parental responsibility.

I recall a mom calling me one winter at one of our indoor sports complexes, complaining that we were still open despite the snow. I explained to her that it had just started snowing, and we didn't know how much it would affect the roads. Her daughter was due to play in a game in the morning, and the mom wanted us to close so she didn't have to drive in the weather. I remember her telling me that I would be held responsible for anything that happened to her or her child on the way to the game.

I calmly explained to her that I would not be responsible. I was doing my job as required by my company. It was ultimately her decision to get into that car with her child. If she felt it was dangerous, then it shouldn't matter if we were open or closed. She should stay home and do what she felt was best for her family. If she thought that it was dangerous, but risked it for a kids' game, then that was her choice.

You choose how important sports are to your family. If you ever see or believe that your child is under threat or in real danger, it's your responsibility to remove them from that situation. If you use your best judgment and always keep in mind that it's just a kids' game, you'll be okay.

As parents, we must acknowledge that we are emotional beings who can become deeply invested in sports. People love sports, and when it comes to youth sports, all the emotions are multiplied exponentially because of how deeply we care for our kids. Far more potent than sports is a parent's love for their child. When we have a child, that child becomes our world. Every parent knows that no book or manual can prepare us for every aspect of parenting. Parenting is the most rewarding and challenging responsibility in our lives. As parents, we must walk a fine line between protecting our children and preparing them for life's challenges. And the tricky part is that we never really know how we're doing. There are no guidelines to tell us whether we should focus more on discipline or emotional support. We receive no weekly report cards to help us decide whether to talk to our child or give them space. There's no signal telling us when to push or when to pull back. Parenting is challenging, confusing, and both incredibly rewarding and deeply frustrating.

Parents underestimate their importance in youth sports.

As adults, we need to show our children how to handle the challenging situations that life presents. This book will help you understand the basics of youth sports and provide strategies to make sure your family has a positive sports experience. It gives you what you need to develop a plan to navigate the emotional environment of youth sports. It will then be your responsibility to follow and uphold it with your family.

This book can serve as a tool. If used properly, it can send a message to everyone that it is time to address problematic behavior in youth sports. It conveys that we understand how emotional youth sports can be, but enough is enough. We need a safe, enjoyable environment for kids that is protected, even from ourselves. Please share this message. The more grounded and responsible adults there are at games, the better we can work together to stop unbalanced, harmful behavior. If you encounter a difficult parent, consider sending them a copy or slipping one under their windshield wiper. You never know; you might save a child from the antics of out-of-control parents on the sidelines and protect their sports experience.

Thank you,
Petronio Morillo
"Coach Pete"

Why Join
Youth Sports?

In today's technology-driven world, encouraging kids to play outside with peers is more important than ever. Youth sports are fun and offer an excellent way for kids to make friends and be active. Numerous studies show that children who participate in sports tend to perform better academically, feel more confident, and are less likely to face common adolescent issues. Life can be tough for kids. They often feel unsure, isolated, and insecure. Sports provide children with direction and offer them teammates, coaches, and friends to support and guide them, helping them stay on the right path.

Practice sessions take time, which keeps kids moving and busy. Kids enjoy playing games, and sports can motivate them to behave well so they can participate. Sports also teach kids about leadership, communication, physical fitness, and personal responsibility. As children develop in their sports, they gain more advanced life skills, including leadership, effective pressure management, and efficient time management.

Sports teach kids to work for and earn what they want. While the primary goal may be to have fun with friends, they quickly realize that without effort, they won't improve. Winning should never be the most important thing, but everyone knows it feels better to win than to lose. Kids in sports will naturally want to improve and win more games than they lose. Players will be asked to lead by example, work together, make in-formed decisions, and pursue shared goals. Youth sports are an excellent place for kids to learn about pressure, but without the serious real-world consequences.

Many children develop a passion for sports. It's been said that passion is the spice of life, and in a world where our daily routines often focus on chores and duties rather than on activities we love, we should encourage our kids to discover what they are passionate about. Finding activities that bring them joy and make them feel alive is essential. There are many ways to cultivate creativity and soulful pleasure, such as painting, writing, cooking, sculpting, acting, and exploring. For some, sports can serve that purpose.

Youth sports experiences can benefit families and create lifelong memories. I highly recommend sports for kids, provided they are enjoyable, safe, and properly managed by responsible adults. Sports offer so much to kids that it is impossible to list all the ways they benefit, but the three primary reasons parents should encourage their kids to participate in sports are for the three "F's." Fun, Friends, and Fitness. These are the most common and purest reasons, and it's essential to keep them at the heart of your family's priorities.

Fun!

I have participated in sports at both the youth and adult levels, and I can confidently say that kids get it right. Adult sporting events are frequently filled with mean-spirited, violent behavior, but give a three-year-old a ball and they will have fun. I have seen adult softball games turn into fistfights, referees chased out of stadiums, and riots incited over sports. There's something about sports that makes some people think they can act without any accountability for their behavior. Even in professional sports where players earn millions, you see violent, disgraceful behavior. How many times have you watched a professional football scrimmage and seen the players get into a fight? We've even seen race car drivers get out of their cars to fight each other. I ran indoor sports complexes for 20 years, and nothing was worse than a grown adult yelling at me about a referee's bad call during a Wednesday night coed volleyball league. I cannot tell you how many irresponsible, out-of-control adults we dealt with over those two decades.

It is one thing for adults to take sports too seriously, but when it comes to youth sports, it's time for us to step back and act responsibly. Parents and coaches must realize that they are there to support the kids as they play a game and have fun. Unlike the real world, pressure, setbacks, and failures in sports shouldn't upset the apple cart.

I recently attended the wedding of one of my former players and had the opportunity to sit down with some of my old players. The players were in their thirties, and I hadn't seen many of them since they left high school. As we sat around sharing old stories, I noticed that soccer games didn't come up, and not a single score was mentioned. Their favorite memories included the State Cup game that ended in a doughnut war, wrapping my dad's truck in toilet paper at overnight camp, and tournament weekends spent with friends and family. They went on and on about going to movies, birthday parties, and hanging out together. They didn't remember the scores of any of the games and didn't care to either.

Kids love games, and families who remember that it's just a kid's game are usually the happiest. Young athletes won't remember the scores of the games unless you do. What they should remember are the fun moments practicing, playing, and being with friends and family. Your kids will cherish the fun, family support, and lessons learned from playing their sport. Youth sports can be fantastic for kids and should be protected. You can do your part by never losing the FUN!

Friends!

We are more connected to each other than ever before, but face-to-face social interaction has reached an all-time low. Kids who don't experience positive social interactions with their peers will be at a disadvantage later in life. While some children seem destined for the stage at birth, many are shy and unsure about social interactions, especially in busy environments. Good social skills aren't innate. They need to be learned and developed in a safe environment. Sports benefit these kids because teammates become friends, and good relationships build confidence. Everyone needs a few good friends.

Sporting environments provide opportunities to develop social skills, make friends, and participate in group discussions. Sports promote teamwork, leadership, and conflict resolution. Being part of a team feels special. Working together toward a shared goal fosters positive and trusting relationships. Making good friends is essential for everyone. Friends share losses and celebrate wins together. Players learn to work together as a team and make sacrifices for one another. Healthy, positive relationships lay the foundation for a happy life.

When your child joins a sports team, they can build lifelong friendships. Many players attend the same schools and play on multiple teams together, making those friendships all the more special. Some teammates even decide to attend the same college. College sports are typically the culmination of most sports careers. For those who choose this path, college sports provide young adults with teammates and coaches who support them throughout their college years. Coaches will monitor players' grades, fitness, and overall well-being to ensure their optimal development. Teammates will create lifelong memories on and off the field or court.

Sports offer young players numerous advantages, but friendships are the most valuable. I have old teammates who are still dear friends today, and I see the same with many of my former players. The network of support and friendship built through sports can be an invaluable lifelong asset to a child.

Fitness!

The third key aspect of sports is fitness. Young athletes develop healthy habits, including regular exercise, balanced diets, and maintaining physical fitness. Today's tech-heavy world causes kids to spend hours sitting on their phones. Often, this leads to adults sitting or standing at work for eight hours a day, which is brutal on their health. Athletic environments naturally encourage kids to train and learn new skills. Kids quickly see the connection between physical fitness and ability and strive to stay fit. Young people involved in sports often grow into adults who understand the importance of maintaining their health and continuing to exercise.

Teaching young people the importance of

fitness, healthy eating, and overall health care is more essential than ever. Regular activity benefits the body, mind, and spirit. Having a young athlete in the family can inspire everyone to adopt a healthier lifestyle. This can range from avoiding unhealthy, processed foods and beverages to maintaining regular exercise routines. Healthy living habits benefit everyone in the family.

Summary

Whether you're considering youth sports or are already involved, the three F's of Fun, Friends, and Fitness are solid, and you can build upon them. If your young player goes out there mainly to enjoy themselves, you're on the right path. As players grow into their sports, the pull to stray from the core elements of Fun, Friends, and Fitness increases, but you cannot let them slip away. If you lose any of these key elements or find that your priorities are changing, you need to stop and reassess immediately.

The vast majority of parents start with good intentions, but it's surprising how often a favorable scenario turns sour. What should be enjoyable for the entire family quickly gets overshadowed by the pressure and expectations tied to the simplest success metrics, like a scoreboard. Don't let this happen to your family. Adults supporting and participating in youth sports must do everything they can to remember that this is about the kids.

Whenever you see your child out there, ask yourself three questions.

1. **Is my child having fun?**
2. **Are they making friends?**
3. **Are they exercising and progressing?**

If the answer to all three is yes, then you are on the right track!

Outside
the Lines

How Did We Get Here?

Throughout human history, sporting events have fascinated us. Ancient horse racing in the desert and gladiatorial combat at the Colosseum both captured the public's imagination. It's often said that sports can capture our attention so thoroughly that they can be used to subdue entire populations. Sports draw us into the drama and excitement of competition, and we love it. As long as human society has existed, sports and competitions have been integral to it. Professional sports excel at cultivating fan loyalty by capitalizing on our passion for sports and our tendency to form emotional attachments.

For many of us, sports carry strong emotional meaning. Many of us remember going to ball games with friends or watching hockey games with our dads, and we cherish those memories. As adults, many of us have taken our kids to sporting events. I have heard of families saving for years to take their kids to a World Cup or a World Series game. It is because of moments like these that sports often hold a unique and cherished place in our hearts.

Unfortunately, professional sports also allow for fan behavior that borders on fanaticism, which can be dangerous. You don't have to look far to find a die-hard professional sports fan. Sports draw us in by satisfying our basic human need for entertainment, excitement, drama, and the lure of conquest. Sometimes sports motivate people to behave in ways they wouldn't otherwise. I recently heard of a super fan who spent time and money buying and replacing the labels on hundreds of blue flares with red labels. He then sold them to a rival team that was red, and when the fans lit them inside the stadium, blue smoke filled the air instead of the expected red. It was a clever trick, and all done out of loyalty to a sports team. I see videos of shirtless fans out in freezing temperatures in places like Buffalo and Boston. People paint themselves, and students storm the court in excited, joyful celebrations. Sports do more than draw a crowd—they captivate and trigger us.

There are boundaries for appropriate behavior, and those boundaries are often crossed in the name of sports. When fan behavior becomes fanatical behavior, we enter a danger zone. We have all seen fans yelling at each other, fighting, or even rioting over games. In 1968, El Salvador and Nicaragua actually went to war after a couple of World Cup Qualifying matches got out of hand. People will do all sorts of crazy things in support of their favorite professional sports teams.

Tragically, the inappropriate adult behavior found at professional sporting events has infiltrated youth sports. On the sidelines and in the stands around the world, parents are displaying fanatical behavior at youth sporting events. I have seen parents storm off in the middle of their child's game, as if they had bought a ticket. Young players are criticized and attacked for how they played the game. Teenage officials are being verbally and sometimes physically abused as if they were full-grown adults. Fanatics at professional sports are bad enough, but when it happens at kids' games, something must be done.

The vast majority of sports parents start with the right intentions and priorities but then lose their way. Adults are emotional beings, but we have been conditioned to hide and control our emotions. And yet, there are certain areas where our passions and emotions can easily get the best of us. One of the biggest is when it comes to our children. I remember breaking down in tears when my son graduated from high school. I didn't expect it at all. I didn't want to embarrass him, but I was overwhelmed with emotion as I watched him walk across the stage. The bottom line is that we love our kids, and so our hearts go with them.

Parental behavior that goes outside the line is a problem rooted in human nature. We are highly emotional creatures, quick to react through our automatic fight-or-flight response system. Sports is an unpredictable environment that is difficult to prepare for, leaving us vulnerable to emotional overreactions. Youth sports take a potentially volatile environment and put our kids right in the middle of it. When that happens, the fight-or-flight response is triggered, and we are immediately ready to fight for our children. This puts parents at risk of taking the game outside the lines and away from the kids.

Youth sports combine two areas where we experience strong emotional reactions: the world of sports and our children. Proper management of youth sports is necessary to prevent emotional overreactions and potential embarrassment for our families and ourselves. We deeply care about our children. Our love for them makes it hard to let them face criticism and failure. We need to recognize and accept that we are susceptible to emotional overreactions when it comes to sports and our kids. Acknowledging this vulnerability helps us take the right approach to managing our behavior.

Over the years, I have noticed three major pitfalls that players and more often parents fall into: **emphasizing results over effort, overinvesting in their sport, and runaway expectations.** All of these contribute to the pressure on the players. These common pitfalls are interconnected and, if not addressed, tend to reinforce one another.

Emphasizing Results Over Effort

A common problem in youth sports is focusing on results over effort. Focusing on wins, records, divisions, leagues, or championships is a mistake. Those are results and are normally outside of a player's control. The only thing a player has control over is their level of effort. They cannot control the outcome of matches, the weather, the track, the field, or their opponent. They can only control how much effort they put forth.

I remember talking to a young player named

Yasmine, who had recently switched teams. I am close with her father, and he called me worried about how she was adjusting to her new team. They had won her first tournament, but she was feeling low. When I spoke with her, she admitted she felt like she hadn't done "enough" to earn her winner's medal. When I asked what she thought she needed to do to "earn" her medal, she focused on two things: a starting position and scoring goals. In her mind, because she hadn't started or scored a goal, she didn't contribute enough. This is a typical case of kids focusing on results rather than effort.

The fastest way to discontent is focusing on results over effort. Yasmine was brand-new to the team, and she played defense. If her measure of success was scoring or starting, it was going to be a difficult season for her. I helped her see that those results were not how she should measure herself. Her focus should have been on how hard she tried to help her team succeed. If she had been focused on her effort, she would have been happy because she tried her best. That was all she could do.

Game outcomes, goals, or team records depend on many variables. No single player can be responsible for all of them, but every player is accountable for how much effort they put in for themselves and their team. That's why emphasizing effort is so crucial for players. We want to reward effort, not hope for results. A player's or a team's performance on any given day depends on many factors, such as mood, sleep, and nutrition. Players may underperform if they have issues with a parent or a friend. Sometimes, a team or player has an off day. These are just a few factors that can influence results, so it's unfair for one player to carry all the responsibility for the results of a game. Recognizing overall effort is the best way for our players to see the value of their performance. If they gave their best, then no one, not even themselves, can ask for more.

Overinvesting in Youth Sports

As I grew into coaching, I found myself seeking a way to help parents and coaches protect kids from the internal pressures they may face. It is critical for parents to set clear limits on the importance and the amount of energy they invest in their kids' sports. If a player ever feels pressured, stressed, or anxious about a sport, you as the parent must step in. Sit your player down and figure out why they are feeling the way they are feeling. Ask your child why they are having such strong feelings about a game.

It is essential to determine whether the pressure or stress is coming from within your child or from external sources, such as coaches, parents, teammates, or the level of play.

During all conversations with your child, make it clear that there is a healthy level of caring about a game. We want them to care and try, but most importantly, to enjoy their sports experience. Be aware of and address any external sources of stress by speaking with the coach. If your child is putting too much pressure on themselves and feeling anxious, talk to them about their fears and help them realize that consequences in sports are not nearly as scary as they might seem.

Sports require a strong commitment from everyone involved. Players must dedicate time and effort to participate, which includes attending practices and games. Often, extra effort, such as working out on their own, is also necessary. Children have busy schedules with school and homework taking up much of their time. Dedicating another ten to fifteen hours a week to sports can be difficult. I have always believed that sports are worth the investment, but everyone's life is different, and only you and your child can decide how much a sport should cost your family in terms of time and effort. No game should be too expensive for your family.

Beyond your time and financial investments is the emotional and mental dedication we give to sports. If left unchecked, kids are likely to care too much and invest too much emotionally. Kids are emotional beings who care about everything, so without proper guidance, they could easily become overly invested emotionally in sports.

I remember when my team lost in the State Cup after we hit a post in stoppage time, and then a roller slipped through my goalkeeper's legs. We were just inches from reaching the semi-final, and I knew every single one of my players could see my disappointment. I was emotionally overinvested in winning a State Cup Championship, and it was painfully obvious. Every parent and player on my team shared the same feeling. It was my disappointment that fueled theirs. Because I was triggered, I couldn't give my players the level of support they needed when they needed it.

Over time, I learned to control my reactions better and became more adept at staying emotionally balanced, but the pull to react remained. It is so important to remember that while we can be emotional, our actions and reactions matter a great deal to our kids. It is natural for children to get overexcited. They are kids, and it's about them, so it's expected. However, as adults, it is our responsibility to set a good example for all children.

Sports provide many benefits and their importance grows, the more we invest in them. We need to be careful about how much emotional investment we allow our kids to make and how much importance they place on sports. A good situation can turn bad if kids become too invested in something as unpredictable as sports.

I remember an early game in my career when my team was still learning the offside trap. For those unfamiliar, an offside trap in soccer involves the whole back line moving together. That day, my two centerbacks just weren't in sync. The backline kept conceding goals as we struggled to organize ourselves. Once the game was almost over and we had lost, I pulled my two centerbacks off and told them we couldn't get it working today, but we'd work on it at practice. The disappointment was evident in all three of us.

A few hours later, I was at home thinking about how to improve my backline when I received a call from one of the centerbacks' mothers. She called because her daughter had been upset since the game. Her daughter believed that our loss was entirely her fault because the offside trap hadn't worked. She was a talented young player who al-

ways gave her best at every practice, and she was overinvested in succeeding. I quickly realized that the real issue was not her role in the game but her emotional and mental well-being. She was giving too much importance to the sport. After a positive conversation where I explained that the game wasn't worth her being upset all day, she and her mother felt better.

I then checked on my other centerback, worried she might be upset as well. I talked with her and her father, and to my surprise, her reaction was the total opposite of her teammate's. She felt totally fine after the game. In her words, she said that "they had not played well and lost badly." And while she wasn't happy about it, she was okay after the game.

This incident has stayed with me over the years because it raised a question in my mind. Why did the two players respond completely differently? I knew both sets of parents, and they were wonderful, caring people. I had spoken with both kids at the same time, and they had played together, so they shared the same experience. Why did one player walk away feeling fine while the other was burdened with such a heavy sense of responsibility for our breakdown? The answer was that the two players invested differently in the game. Kids don't know how much to invest emotionally or how even to consider the issue. One player was overinvested emotionally and upset, while the other was solidly grounded and perfectly happy. Over the years, I have come to realize that if we allow children to choose how much they care or how to use their time, they will care too much or give too much, which can lead to stress and pressure to perform. That is not what any of us want in youth sports.

Overinvesting occurs when players practice every waking minute or work out excessively. Parents have told me they have taken their kids to practice even though their children were behind on schoolwork. I have also heard about kids missing important family events for soccer practice or practicing while on vacation. Doing things like this gives kids the impression that sports are more important than schoolwork or family obligations. This is not the message we want to send to our kids. Overinvesting can turn a child's game into a pressure-filled environment that is unsuitable for kids.

Ultimately, many factors influence how much meaning things hold for our children, but youth sports should not cause stress or anxiety. Children shouldn't fear attending practices or lose sleep over games. There should be excitement and anticipation, not fear. The most critical factor in how much your child invests in their sport should be parental input and guidelines. Children don't have the ability to monitor themselves, so without proper parental guidance, kids will care too much.

Watching your kids play is great, but parents don't have much free time, so that must be considered. Overinvesting by parents can lead to player overinvestment, disappointment, anxiety, and pressure. As parents you spend a lot of time and money on their sports. It is challenging to get them to practice. You will see your child trying so hard, and then hear opposing parents cheer as your child's team struggles. It can make your blood boil. It's especially upsetting when people go over the top, cheering, while your child suffers. **Your protective instincts can reveal themselves in powerful ways.** This is where overinvesting can become a serious problem, and adults may react in ways they usually wouldn't.

There was once a nine-year-old boy who was a little phenom. He was small but very skillful, loved playing soccer, and was always trying to impress his father. One season, he showed up after gaining a little weight. It seemed that his parents were going through a nasty divorce, and he was showing signs of distress. His lack of fitness, combined with his small stature, really affected his game. There were tears in his eyes after he got caught from behind on a breakaway. His dad's reaction didn't help, as he had left the field afterwards to wait in the car. That little boy quit soccer after that very game and didn't play again until he was an adult. The emotional investment became too much for him.

Parents are responsible for protecting themselves and their families from overinvesting. It will be a constant give-and-take, so stay vigilant. The draw of sports can be relentless, so parents must be steadfast.

Beware of Runaway Expectations

It's human nature to develop expectations. Expectations, simply put, are our brains using what we know to predict the future. It may sound counterintuitive, but it's true. Our intellect allows us to reason and anticipate outcomes based on the information we gather. Our brains are extraordinary, but as we all know, no one can see the future. It is an automatic function of our brains to make educated guesses about what will happen so we can prepare for it, and it's often wrong.

Expecting things is so natural that we often don't even notice it. For example, if you say, "thank you," you usually expect and then anticipate hearing "you're welcome." If you greet someone with "hello" and get no response, it feels awkward because you expected a reply. Have you ever taken a trip and heard airport staff say, "Enjoy your trip," and you automatically responded, "You too?" You know they aren't going anywhere—they are working. Your brain predicted what you were supposed to say, and it was wrong. It happens all the time, which is why we must be careful. Often, what we expect may cause stress by shaping our standards for success. For example, if you start going to the gym and lose ten pounds in the first month, you may set a standard of success without realizing it. What if you keep the same routine but only lose five pounds the next month? It might feel like you fell short, even though your effort was the same. The reality is that you lost fifteen pounds in two months, which is fantastic! Your unrealistic goals led to feelings of disappointment with your progress.

The real danger in unchecked expectations is that they affect our standards and get out of hand fast. Many parents fail to see how their expectations grow along the way and can be oblivious to when they shift from reasonable to unrealistic. I recall my first year with a team where the parents' expectations were so low that they told me upfront that the girls would never be a Division I team. Two years later, after getting into Division 1, a meeting was held to discuss firing me after we went 0-3 in a preseason tournament. In another three years, that team would win the top division twice and be ranked among the regional top 25.

I once coached a very good girls' team in an indoor futsal league. This team was such that the families had very low expectations from the beginning. However, as the team kept improving and became regionally ranked, expectations around the team grew out of control. I recall playing a team that was clearly outmatched. I spoke with the coach, and he said his team was aware of the skill difference but was just excited to play against us. So, we played the game. After going up by a few goals too quickly, I started imposing passing restrictions and challenging my team to keep the score from getting out of hand. The game ended in a 7-3 victory for our team. After speaking with a grateful coach who saw exactly what we had done, I left the court feeling good about the game. That is, until I ran into a parent's runaway expectations. One of the parents on my team approached me, livid. She was agitated because the parents on the other team had celebrated the game as a victory for their team. One parent had claimed that their team had "hung with a nationally ranked team." She felt embarrassed because she expected us to crush the other team, so their parents would have nothing to cheer about. It was outrageous. Parental expectations hijack our emotions, leaving us without empathy or compassion for the kids. They turn parents into fanatics and create a hostile environment for everyone.

Having expectations is natural. We all have them, but the younger the child, the less reasonable those expectations tend to be. When a young child wants something, they expect to get it immediately. A child's life is relatively easy when their parents provide everything they need. While getting everything effortlessly may seem nice, it doesn't help develop reasonable expectations. Sports are often the first time many kids face an adversity that their parents can't handle for them. They won't always be the fastest or the best. They will make mistakes and face failure from time to time, and that's okay because that is how they will learn to understand their abilities and limitations.

Youth sports provide a unique environment for kids — a place where expectations and standards can be learned and developed without the real-life consequences they will face as adults. A player with runaway expectations will not be able to meet the standards they set for themselves or achieve their goals, which will hurt their confidence. An athlete without confidence is an unhappy and soon-to-be-ex-athlete. Conversely, reasonable expectations lead to reachable standards and achievable goals, helping build a player's confidence. Confidence is vital for athletes. A confident player is a happy player. Happy players will want to keep working and improving.

Feeling disappointed in oneself is common for adults, and when managed well, it teaches us how to set realistic goals. However, too much self-disappointment can become a serious problem. When children start playing a sport, they often lack the experience of setting realistic goals. They attempt to establish standards but may lack the emotional maturity to cope with failing to meet them. What kids expect can become a problem when it leads to unreachable standards and goals, causing a continuous cycle of disappointment. Young adults often expect too much of themselves or a situation, which can lead to disappointment and a loss of confidence.

Elite Player Expectations

Often, it is the parents of elite players who overinvest in sports, leading to runaway expectations. I cannot tell you how many parents have told me they can't keep their kids off the field. Talented players love playing, and setting proper limits won't be easy. However, even elite players need boundaries and a sense of balance. School, grades, chores, family, and their well-being are just a few examples of things that are more important than sports, no matter what level of athlete.

As players age, their wants and opinions become increasingly important, but keep in mind that children are not the best decision-makers. That is why they rely on their parents. If you have a child whose love of the game drives them to become a high-level player, their talent and drive will make them successful. They will be more focused and more interested, and the system will also push them to play more. However, this often leads to burnout. Parents must be the stopgap. Even the best players can overdo it if you let them. Sports are designed to showcase and identify gifted athletes, so the interest will be there; they do not have to push themselves to the extreme. Even elite athletic academies that are aware of the high risk of burnout struggle to retain their players year after year.

Parents of top players often worry that

setting firm boundaries might stop their child from reaching their full potential. However, they need to understand that the chance of their child becoming a professional athlete is very low. The odds of a college athlete making it to the pros in basketball, soccer, or football are around 1 percent. Having coached some top-level players, I can say that truly exceptional players will stand out and succeed, but burnout from internal and external pressure is much more common than "making it." The pressure on elite athletes can be extreme. In many cases, the pressure comes from within the player, but often it can be traced to parental expectations of excellence. Elite talent is rare, and making it to a professional league is even rarer, so this should not be a primary goal or worry for any parent.

Summary

Focusing on results over effort, overinvesting, and having runaway expectations are three sure-fire ways to take the joy out of youth sports. As we discussed earlier, our culture has fostered an unchecked fanaticism around sports. Unfortunately, what was once behavior confined to professional sports has now entered youth sports. Adult behavior has not only infected youth sports, but our children are following our bad example. We must change the culture for the sake of our young people. Parents are critical to this shift. We must prepare intellectually and emotionally so we can be the best parents possible and show our youth how to manage themselves.

Keeping It
Between the Lines

Sports naturally come with excitement and pressure; parents do not need to add any more. No matter what level of competition your kids may play, it should be fun because, at the end of the day, all youth sports are recreational. Recreation is defined as any activity that amuses us, stimulates us, and renews our health and spirit. Youth sports should do that for all involved. It is the responsibility of the adults involved to ensure the safety and security of every player, not just their own. Parents should remain focused so they can keep pressure within the lines of the field or court. Parents should never be a source of pressure

Now, let's talk about your role as a parent. It is the most important and influential part of this entire experience. It might not always seem that way, but it's the truth. Your child will likely have several coaches whom they will admire, but you are their parent. You are the person whom they should depend on and trust the most. As parents, you must cherish that trust and avoid living your dreams through your children, which is a more common scenario than you might think.

Parents need to be mindful of their priorities by focusing on effort over results, avoiding overinvestment by setting the right tone, and managing expectations. Additionally, parents should be cautious with their words, emotions, and messages. Kids will sometimes need help getting motivated Adults must maintain a broad perspective on their family's situation as they learn to navigate the world of youth sports. Parents must do all that while staying grounded emotionally and setting the right example for their family.

When it comes to protecting their kids, parents can quickly lose control of their emotions. Just like when my son graduated from high school. Every parent has had that moment when their emotions get the better of them. It was emotion that got me into coaching in the first place.

I had a buddy named Coach Rene who asked me to help him at practice. He had a boys' team that was just starting to learn how to play. I recall seeing a kid who was early to practice, trying to learn a step-over. I walked over, helped him get the mechanics right, and then encouraged him to try it in every game situation he could, at practice and at the game that weekend. I told him that the average player must do a move wrong 100 times before they get it right. I saw him trying to get it right, all practice. I knew he would get it soon.

I decided to go to the game that weekend. A few minutes into his second shift out there, he hit the move perfectly and shot past a defender. He was so excited that he forgot where he was going and turned to look for me on the sideline. When his eyes caught mine, his smile beamed straight to my heart. From then on, I knew that coaching was what I wanted to do.

For some of you, sports are the first time you're letting your child go beyond arm's reach. Even if that is not the case, you're allowing your child to play a sport, and there are inherent risks you can't protect them from. No matter your situation, youth sports can be an emotional roller coaster. Few things involving our kids are easy, so we need to be prepared to avoid being caught unaware, as I was while watching my son cross that stage.

While you cannot be out there with them, it is your responsibility to ensure that your child has a positive sports experience. As we grow older, we forget how important our parents were to us when we were children. When we were kids, our parents were our world. We believed that they would protect us from harm and provide what we needed. We wanted to look up to them, learn from them, and trust that they would be there for us. As children, a simple look of pride or disapproval from our parents could send shivers down our spines. As a parent, you must never forget that you are the most critical person in your child's life, and your words and actions carry the most weight. If you want your kids to keep their composure, then you must keep yours.

Parents are the lifeblood of their child's sports journey and must wear many hats. You are their source of unconditional love, their shepherd, mentor, and fan. Here are some responsibilities that every parent should keep at the forefront of their minds.

Set the Tone and Stay Grounded

Parents are the primary role models for their children, and it is their responsibility to set the right tone, support their efforts, and maintain an even keel. These three things are interconnected. Once a parent finds the right tone, they must help their child while maintaining a consistent approach. Staying grounded and in control is essential, but it can easily become complicated in the world of youth sports.

Parents must set the right tone for their child's sports experience from the start. We need to be the adults we want our children to become because our kids will follow our example. Our children look up to us from the earliest moments. They learn from what we say, what we don't say, and how we act. They will walk our walk and talk our talk, so be mindful. If we focus on winning, they will too. If we tell them they should be a point guard, they'll want to be one. If we tell them they are better than everyone else on the team or that they are the weakest player, they will believe us. It's a hard truth to accept, but parents are their kids' most influential and dedicated teachers. They know what we teach them, and they don't know what we don't teach them. Parents must remain grounded and in control to be a good role model for their player.

A parent's job isn't to be the loudest in the crowd. It's not about controlling the referee, coach, or the game. All we need to do is focus on our child, their team, and their coach. Kids want us to be involved by watching, so we can see when they succeed. They also want us to watch when they don't do so well, so we can reassure them that it's not so bad.

There's nothing wrong with getting excited over your kids' sports. I loved celebrating with my teams. However, parents must remember that this is about the kids. Your excitement shouldn't overshadow the kids. They want you to be excited, but not overly so; that's embarrassing. We all know how easily kids can be embarrassed by their parents. Some of us enjoy embarrassing our kids, but we must choose our moments wisely. Youth sports are for them and about them. Let them get excited, and you go along for the ride. Stay cool, calm, and collected out there—that's what's best for our children.

Parents must understand that kids will interpret their levels of excitement and engagement either way. If you look disinterested, this can make a kid feel inadequate. In contrast, getting overexcited can cause a child to believe their performance is critical to your joy. It is a thin line, but parents must find and hold it.

A parent's role is to prepare and equip their child with the tools needed to handle life's challenges. Youth sports will test your child's ability to manage their emotions. They will feel excited when they score and upset when they make mistakes. Players will face adversity, which will push them into emotional highs and lows. Parents will be dragged along on this journey, but they must stay grounded. This way, their kids can see that, no matter what happens, their parents are in control.

Parents who struggle to handle the emotional pressure of sports often let their kids down or embarrass them. Parents who remain in control of their emotions set a good example for their children and can adequately support and guide them. To achieve this, parents need to strike a balance between being in control and showing their excitement. This will not be easy, and you may need to speak to your child before every practice and game to ensure everyone is on the same page.

A well-grounded parent who understands their role can provide both firm boundaries and consistent support. Never forget that your words and actions have a significant impact on your children. You never know when a child will seek your love and support. Keeping your reactions and emotions in check during games prepares you to be there when they need you. It is your responsibility to keep sports in perspective for your family.

Be Present

When your child is giving it their all, it is your

job as a parent to be there and to be present. There is little difference between a child not seeing their parent in the stands at all and seeing them up there staring at their phone. Our kids need us to be there for them. That means watching your child as they give their all to impress the person whose opinion they value the most—you. Being there means catching your kid's eye after they make a great play. It means giving a smile when they look for you. In case you forgot, that means the world to a kid. We all know that missing your child's practices and games for work is often necessary, but missing work for your kids is also essential. They need you, and nothing sends a clearer message of what's more important than never showing up to Little League.

Youth sports require a significant amount of effort, time, and money, but your kids are well worth it. When your kids are trying their best out there, they are doing it for themselves, their team, and YOU! So don't miss it!

Maintain Balance

Parents should be ready to guide their children in managing their investment in sports. Kids need to be taught that there's an acceptable level of care and excitement over a game, and that's where they should stay. Adults must set and hold firm boundaries on overinvesting by their children.

There was once a kid who ran through my child development program like a superstar! I mean, this kid loved playing soccer, and it showed. His father told me that they couldn't get him to do anything else. He wouldn't do homework until it got dark outside. He took a ball on vacation and played so much beach soccer the first day that he could barely walk for the rest of the trip. The father was so proud of how much his son played, and swore his boy was going to be the ONE! I warned him about burnout. His coaches and even his wife warned him, but he wouldn't listen.

A few years later, I saw him at a soccer field. He told me his son had stopped playing altogether and now never stops playing video games. His head dropped in disappointment as he admitted that his son didn't want to play anymore. I felt bad for him, but this is the danger of overinvesting in sports.

The same principles of overinvesting must apply to adults, so we will start by making sure we don't overinvest either. Supporting a young athlete is a lot of work. It means driving to practices and games, volunteering for team duties, and attending team events. It also includes paying for equipment, coaches, and tournaments. These are part of every youth sport, which is why we must stay alert to how we feel as we support our child's emotional and physical journey.

If you devote too much emotion, time, effort, or money to youth sports, you may lose sight of your priority as a positive, supportive parent. You're not investing in sports for financial gain, which is good because the chances of that are very slim. Instead, you're investing in your child's enjoyment and growth. That remains true at any level, so never invest more than your family can afford financially, emotionally, or in actual time and effort.

Keep a Realistic Perspective

Runaway expectations are rampant in sports. It is so bad that often speaking expectations out loud is taboo in sports. In baseball, teammates won't even talk to a pitcher on a no-hitter. When watching hockey, we were not even allowed to say the word "shutout" until the game was over. Expecting it before you get it is a surefire way to jinx it! Runaway expectations are considered very dangerous by athletes.

Any time we let our expectations get out

of hand, we risk creating problems. This is especially true in youth sports. Parents naturally have aspirations, dreams, and expectations for their kids, but they shouldn't impose those expectations on their child's performance or sports career. It isn't fair. Youth sports are for the kids, so it's essential to manage their expectations and help them set realistic standards and goals. If you impose your own hopes, dreams, and expectations, you may change the entire dynamic of the experience. It may not be easy, but we must set our egos aside.

Managing your personal ambitions and expectations for your child may not come naturally. We are emotional beings, and youth sports can be a complex emotional landscape. You'll see your family make sacrifices for your child's practices and games. Siblings may be forced to tag along, and family time will be sacrificed. You'll think about how much time and effort your child invests. You'll watch fellow parents and the coaches all pulling for the team, and you will empathize with them. So much effort goes into youth sports, and naturally, we will expect all that effort to pay off. What we must remember is that effort and desire do not always yield results in ways we might expect. This reality can lead to disappointment. Parents must keep their expectations in check for their children's benefit.

Once, a mom asked me if I could guarantee her daughter would play at the University of North Carolina like Mia Hamm. I explained that UNC might only accept a few players each year, and every female soccer player in the world wanted to go there. Mia Hamm was extremely popular at the time and had recently graduated from UNC, boosting U.S. women's soccer worldwide. I also told the mom that many kids quit soccer in their teens due to pressure. Lastly, I mentioned that since her daughter was only twelve, it might be best to wait and see if she even wanted to play college soccer. Her daughter was a good player and a female soccer player in the nineties, which meant she loved Mia Hamm. However, she wasn't thinking about her college soccer career at twelve. Ultimately, her mom chose another coach who claimed he could give her daughter the best chance to get into UNC. Can you imagine the pressure this creates for a kid?

Parents need to support players as they learn to determine their own standards for growth and development. Parental guidance is essential, but we must not confuse our child's goals with our own. This could lead to confusion and disappointment, which we definitely want to avoid with young athletes. Varying expectations cause inconsistent measures of progress and different standards for success. If you fall into this trap with your child, it increases the likelihood that they will feel they have let you down. That's a tough feeling for a child, and we want to prevent it.

A common issue in youth sports between parents and kids involves how playing time is shared. When you and your child disagree on how much they should play, problems can emerge. If your child is content with their playing time, but you complain to the coach because you expect more, it implies that your child's effort isn't enough for you.

It's important to know that, beyond league rules, the coach decides who plays. In many less competitive leagues, playing time is supposed to be evenly shared among all players, but this can change as you move up in competition. This is a common problem that we will explore in more detail later in the book; however, open and honest communication with your child will help ensure that your expectations and standards are aligned. Parents want to be involved in their child's development, but they cannot impose their expectations on them. Stay focused on your child and prioritize the Three F's—Fun, Friends, and Fitness—and you will stay on track.

Look For the Effort

Focusing on results rather than effort is something adults often do unconsciously. We frequently focus on the goal or result and overlook the effort it takes to get there. When you watch your child try to stand for the first time, you feel disappointed each time they try and fall, but you celebrate when they stand. You sit anxiously when they struggle to speak, and then run around the room celebrating when they say their first word. From birth, you've supported your child's efforts to reach milestones, but you saved the celebration for when their efforts paid off. Once they start sports, you're eager to cheer for their success, but success is measured differently in youth sports. In youth sports, effort always pays off, but it doesn't always show up on the scoreboard. Understanding that reality changes everything.

Youth sports are like a Broadway show; you see the performance at games, but much more goes into the production. Parents don't see all the effort players put forth every day, but we must respect it. How hard a player or team tries is not always reflected in standings, goals, or game results. Like a performance, the players' efforts are the only things they truly have control over. Many factors can influence the result of a game, and sometimes the better team loses, but that doesn't lessen the effort those kids put in. Keep your focus on the players' effort, and you will always be proud of them.

Let Go of Judgments

A central problem we encounter in youth sports is that parents rarely take their own biases into account. Most parents are biased and see their children through rose-colored glasses. They believe that their kids are better than they really are. In contrast, some parents see their children through a far too critical lens. This comes with the serious problem of a child never living up to their parents' standards, which can lead to self-esteem issues. The vast majority of parents are somewhere in between, but we all have biases. That's why parent's opinions, standards, and priorities should take a distant back seat. Parents should leave the coaching and critiquing to coaches. Your child, your coach, and your team will appreciate it.

I once had a parent on my team who would tell me that her son was the fastest kid on the team. Every time I saw her, she would ask why I had the quickest kid on the bench. She couldn't see the irony in her question.

Why would any coach keep any player out of the game if that player would help the team?

Adults routinely accuse coaches of doing this, but it never makes sense. Coaches want to win games, too. From my experience, if the team's objective is to win, then the coach will put the players on the field who can best reach that end.

I recall the day the mother of our "fastest" player showed up to watch practice. She didn't attend many practices, so I finished the session with a few races. We did some quick sprints followed by a longer recovery drill to test endurance. Her son finished in the middle of the pack in the sprints and was among the last to finish the fitness race. I thought that would settle the matter. I was wrong. The very next time I saw her, she asked why my fastest player didn't play more. I wondered if she had seen the race after practice, and she explained that her son wasn't feeling well during that session. Nothing, not even witnessing it herself, convinced her otherwise.

Biased parents may find it hard to judge their children's performance fairly. I've lost count of how many times I've talked with parents, defending myself over player decisions, while trying not to say outright that their kid just wasn't as good as they believed. On the other hand, I have also had a few too many instances where I was forced to defend a player from a negatively biased parent who continually tore down their kid. Parents are biased—I'm a parent too. We must recognize and accept it so that we can trust our players and coaches as they deserve.

I remember a game we had to win to stay in Division 1. The girls had worked really hard all season and were desperate not to be relegated to Division 2. In the past few games, my holding midfielder had struggled. She had some things going on at home that were distracting her, and it showed in the games. In this final game, I gave another player a chance, and they performed well. We won, and the team and parents were thrilled, all except one parent—the mother of the girl who had lost her starting spot. She approached me and yelled at me in front of her daughter, who moments ago had been in a joyful celebration with her teammates. She knew exactly how many minutes her daughter had played and wanted everyone to see that it was unacceptable to her. She stormed away, pulling her daughter by the arm. The child looked humiliated, and I never saw them again. We had failed to meet the mom's expectations. It never occurred to her that the other player was better that day or that her daughter was happy for her team. It was easier for her to think I was wrong.

As adults, we must face our issues to manage them. Admitting your bias may not be easy, but it is the best way to manage it.

Be a Motivator

I often get asked by parents what to do if a player isn't motivated to try harder. This is a tricky situation. Early in my coaching career, I cut a player because she said she saw no reason to work harder after failing to regain her starting spot. That decision remains one of my biggest regrets. What I didn't realize at the time was that she wasn't motivated because I hadn't inspired her. She felt like she was failing, and I let her believe that—this feeling of failure drained her motivation. The truth is, she had improved, but I hadn't taken the time to let her know about her progress.

When a player enjoys playing, they are self-motivated but will still need encouragement from time to time. If a player is never motivated, they are probably playing for the wrong reasons. Most kids fall somewhere in the middle, but if a kid is forced to play a sport, nothing and no one can truly motivate them. It's unreasonable to expect anyone to be motivated to do something they are being forced to do. Parents can force kids to play sports, but they shouldn't expect them to enjoy or excel at them if that's the case.

Watch Your Words

As parents, we must be mindful of the messages we send to our children. What you say to them matters, and sometimes it's what you don't say that causes the most hurt. If you get too excited, kids might think the game is more important than it really is. Looking disinterested on the sidelines sends the message that you don't care. If you complain about the cost or time commitment, your kids may feel guilty and pressured to perform. Your child needs to understand that the main goal is to have fun, and one way to do that is to hear it from you. If your words and messages focus on the right priorities, your player will remember them.

Parents are human, and we all have our thoughts, feelings, and opinions. If you aren't careful, you can unintentionally send the wrong message, despite having good intentions. For example, I often hear parents motivate their kids with rewards. "Ice cream after the game if we win!" Or, "My dad said, if I score today, he will buy me a new video game!" This is a common mistake by parents and grandparents who don't realize what the kids may be hearing.

The unspoken message says, "If you don't win, then it's not good enough for ice cream!" They imply, "No matter how hard you try or how well you play, no goal means no reward." These kinds of messages imply that if they don't achieve the results the parent expects, they have failed, even if they gave their best effort.

If you get caught up in the drama and excitement, you might lose your way and become a critical parent. Children of critical parents are never happy players. Kids don't want to be criticized by their parents, and if we're honest, most of the time they don't even want to be corrected by their parents. Children are sensitive, and criticism is hardest to take from those closest to us. Who wants to live with a "Parent Critic"?

The truth is that players tend to accept and respond more effectively to critical feedback from coaches. Players expect critical insights from coaches, not from parents, and they definitely don't expect it from someone else's parent. **Please never criticize someone else's child.** That's a big mistake. An adult criticizing someone else' child is the most abhorrent behavior. It harms the kids and can wreck a team environment. Adults, especially parents, should know better.

Kids want and need support from parents,

not criticism. The reason is simple: your words hold a lot of power. You're their parent, and no one wants to disappoint their parents. Criticizing your child's development can hurt more than you might realize. That's why it's important to let kids evaluate their progress and allow coaches to critique players while you focus on setting a positive tone and supporting your child.

Summary

When supporting our kids, it's crucial to stay positive and encouraging. No one ever said parenting would be easy, and sports parents take on a significant load. A parent can be their kid's greatest fan, or a source of anxiety and pressure. Following the advice in this section will help you stay grounded and available for your child when they inevitably need you. Naturally, your kids will seek your opinion, and you should be supportive. The best responses are always positive, honest, and encouraging. No matter where they are or what has happened, always offer them compliments. Even after a poor game or a mistake, parents can still turn things around by saying things like:

1. "You learned an important lesson today, which is great for next time."
2. "Mistakes happen all the time; it's about how you respond. I'm proud of you."
3. "You gave it your best. You're getting better every game!"
4. "I thought you played well today, and I enjoyed watching!"
5. "The good news is that this game is over, and we can get better next week."

You are the parent; you hold the power. Use it wisely.

Finding the
Right Environment

Now that I have outlined the responsibilities that fall on parents who support youth sports, let's move to choosing the right sports environment for your family. A family's sports environment includes their level of competition, club, team, and coach. There are many different types of youth-sport environments, and finding the right one for your child can feel like navigating a carnival fun house. Choose a team environment whose values and behaviors mirror what you instill at home. No matter what level your child plays, sports should never come before family responsibilities and values. Keep your priorities straight and follow the strategy outlined here.

Choosing a League, Club, or Academy

Youth sports fall into one of two structures for organizing their teams. One way to manage a youth sport is to have teams register directly with leagues and be divided by skill level. A league is simply a company that registers teams, reserves fields, and makes divisions and schedules. Conversely, in some sports, such as soccer, teams are affiliated with clubs or academies, such as Liverpool International Youth Academy or FC Bayern International Youth, and register to play in leagues under those clubs. Clubs and academies are companies that focus on team training. They are usually a collection of teams in different age groups that all play under the club umbrella. It is a way of structuring training that builds as teams age. Many clubs will have multiple teams of differing skill levels in each age group. They are convenient ways to organize teams.

There are differences according to the size of the club or academy. Most larger clubs or academies are affiliated with a city, such as Loudon Soccer Club in Loudoun, Virginia, or Potomac SA in Potomac, Maryland. These are large, established organizations with many teams across every age group, designed to offer opportunities for their local families. Smaller clubs or academies are very similar to clubs, but are independent of any city and usually have fewer team options. Independent clubs can provide excellent and personalized service.

The sports world includes many wonderful people dedicated to supporting children; however, as with anything, there are coaches, academies, clubs, and leagues whose only goal is to make money. Most parents start by choosing a sports academy or club. Many are excited when their child is offered a place on a highly ranked team or a "youth professional club" that costs thousands of dollars. Beware of high-pressure clubs or academies that charge a lot, but deliver little. It's well known that people often over-spend on their children and pets, and there are those in the sports world who take advantage of that fact. Most big clubs are genuinely dedicated and structured to create a positive, educational environment for kids, with extras like free clinics or personalized training. Many smaller academies can still offer excellent personal service, but may lack the options and structure of larger clubs. The level of interaction between clubs and teams varies greatly, so it's essential to explore your options.

Level of Competition

Once you have identified the club you want to join, it's time to pick a team. However, you must first ensure that your child starts at the appropriate level of play. The level of competition for your child will depend on their desire to play, skill level, and family priorities. More competition usually means a greater required investment. Youth sports are about having fun and building friendships. While competition is a part of sports, it should never be the primary focus. As a parent, you need to find a balance between what your child wants, what they are capable of, and what your family wants to invest.

When considering which level to start with, the goal should be to place players at a level that challenges them sufficiently and provides a fair opportunity to compete with their teammates. You mustn't begin at too challenging a level. Doing so makes your child a weaker player, who must play catch-up, and nobody wants to start from behind. On the other hand, you don't want to start too low. If your child is significantly better than everyone else, this can slow their development and reduce their enjoyment by making the game too easy.

When selecting your level of play, always keep your own and your child's priorities in mind. I always recommend starting at a lower level and then progressing as the family becomes more comfortable with the level of commitment. High-level sports require a significant financial investment and a large time commitment from families. These commitments often increase over time, so think carefully before jumping onto the fast-moving train of highly competitive sports. I've seen parents become resentful over costs and siblings sleeping on the sidelines during long tournament weekends. Don't get me wrong, I've always worked with highly competitive teams and really enjoyed it. Kids dedicated to excelling in a sport are a joy to work with, but higher levels of play can get expensive.

When determining the right level of competition for your child, always err on the side of caution and choose a level where you know they can compete. Let's assume there are three levels of competition: beginner, intermediate, and most competitive. For a player to start at the highest level of competition, they should be advanced. They usually have had independent coaching, such as by family members or a child development program. Few parents choose to start at this level if their kids aren't confident and skilled. Most players with some experience will want to play at the intermediate level, and those with little to no experience will start at the beginner level.

If your child is currently playing at the wrong level of competition, then you face what I often call the Player's Dilemma. It is essential to note that the Player's Dilemma is common in youth sports. This occurs when a player has a passion for a sport and advances beyond their current team. It creates the dilemma of whether they should leave for a stronger team or stay with friends. I firmly believe that players should make this decision themselves. Choosing to leave behind familiarity and friends is tough. Many talented players face this difficult choice. The only person who knows the best decision is the player, and whatever they choose is the right decision. If they choose a higher-ranked team and succeed, they can always support their friends' team from the sidelines. And if they decide to leave and don't like the new team, they should be able to return. But keep in mind that stability is vital to players as well. Chemistry and camaraderie take time to develop, so team hopping can be detrimental to your child's growth. As always, your child's enjoyment remains the top priority, so this decision is best made together with your child.

Choosing the Right Team

More often than not, it is the coaches and team parents who are responsible for the team environment. When coaches are teachers who genuinely care about their players, and parents maintain cordial, supportive boundaries, the teams are secure, healthy, and welcoming. On the other hand, a team where parents are unwelcoming or parents are hostile toward new teammates reflects an unhealthy environment.

When you join a sports team, the player isn't the only one to consider. Remember, this will affect your entire family. You will meet other parents, and your player's siblings will become friends with the other siblings on the team. The team environment should feel safe, inclusive, and family-friendly. Parents and players should be welcoming to new families. Your family will spend a lot of time in the same places, so you want teams that have a good, wholesome atmosphere.

Aspects of a Positive Team Environment

1. Respect is a value and a practice

Respect should be the foundation of every sports program — a non-negotiable value that every player, coach, and parent upholds. The world would be a different place if we were all taught to respect each other from a young age. We need to show our kids that everyone deserves respect. Children learn by what they see, and if they witness adults disrespecting players, officials, or others, they will think it's acceptable. It's not okay to disrespect someone just because they are young or because you disagree with them. We must teach our kids to behave and to communicate respectfully, or they will grow into disrespectful adults. The sports world is an excellent place for adults and children to practice being respectful, even in challenging situations.

I have seen coaches yell at kids in front of parents who do nothing. I once heard an Academy Director threaten a twelve-year-old with never being allowed to play again. How can a child learn respect if adults are allowed to disrespect them? It's wrong, and I wouldn't hesitate to step onto the field to remove my child from such an environment during a game. Coaches should never disrespect children. Parents shouldn't disrespect the coach, other parents, or kids. This should be a deal breaker for any team. Sports are not more important than a child's well-being or our self-respect. I recommend establishing clear expectations for and with your child.

2. Adults on the team must practice and teach self-discipline

Learning to control oneself is part of growing up and should be emphasized in youth sports. Young people need to know how to listen, follow directions, and manage themselves notwithstanding life's pressures and distractions. We all learn through trial and error how behavior relates to consequences. Youth sports are a natural way to teach this because the consequences for mistakes are often immediate. Staying up late for an early morning game causes players to struggle. Not completing homework on time results in missing practice, which can lead to lost game time. Making mistakes hurts, but they are also lessons in how actions or inactions have repercussions. Learning the cause-and-effect relationship between errors and consequences is an essential step in the maturing process. Likewise, we must teach children self-discipline, so they put that phone down and go practice. Self-discipline will help them get off that couch and do their chores. It is a valuable life skill that coaches and parents should consistently reinforce.

Coaches with self-discipline practice what they preach. If the players are present, then their coaches should also be present. They will start and finish practices on time. They arrive on time and with all their necessary equipment. Lastly, when they are working, they present themselves professionally. I have seen coaches running practice sessions in sandals. Some coaches will stand on the sideline looking like they just rolled out of bed.

The mother of one of my team captains once reprimanded me for arriving at games after warm-ups had begun. My reasoning at the time was that my team was fully capable of warming themselves up and getting going. However, what I didn't see was that my absence put more responsibility on my team captain. A good coach will know that instilling self-discipline in their players starts with the coach.

In a team environment, team parents also serve as role models for how to behave. Suppose parents on your team lack self-discipline and misbehave by screaming and yelling at kids or referees, creating a ruckus on the sidelines, embarrassing their child, or disrespecting the coach. In that case, that is a bad environment for your family.

3. The team shows a good work ethic
When kids start playing sports, they are often

accustomed to their parents providing everything they need with little effort on their part. Sports can be the first time a child has to develop a work ethic to earn something they want. Just as in life, the skills needed to excel at sports don't come free, and they don't come easily. Your kids will have to work at their sport to enjoy it. Finding a team with a strong work ethic in its players will benefit your child.

To excel in a sport, players must dedicate time, demonstrate discipline, and work diligently. Laziness is a negative trait for an aspiring athlete. Athletes must continue to work and improve or face the consequences. Players should quickly learn that skill in sports doesn't come easily—instead, they will have to work for it. Every player brings their own unique skills to their sport. Some skills are immediately apparent, such as exceptional size, speed, or strength. Other skills can be just as essential, if not more so, but are less visible—such as intelligence, the right attitude, and a strong work ethic. While having a few outstanding skills helps, every player must do one thing I call the great equalizer. The path to greatness begins with a drive to work.

Coaches should demonstrate a strong work ethic by arriving on time, being prepared, and being present at each session. A good coach finds the best way to motivate their players to work hard and enjoy the process, without overtraining them. The word "work" may send a kid running in the opposite direction, so coaches need to frame it as a path to success. A good coach will have players eager to work because they are excited about improving.

You do not want a tyrannical coach who forces his players to work through fear and or intimidation.

I once saw a coach running a team of high school boys up and down this hill for nearly an hour. I walked over and asked what the team had done to deserve such a tough fitness session. I remember the man laughing as he said, "Nothing. This is our first practice, and I am going to run them until someone quits or throws up." When I asked him why, he said, "I want to see who really wants to be on the team."

This isn't the kind of coach I would want for my child. He was essentially punishing his players for wanting to play soccer. Running them into exhaustion to see who wants to be there would only make every player want to be somewhere else. Find a coach who knows how to demonstrate and teach a good work ethic.

4. You want a team that prioritizes teamwork

Life is about the relationships we build, and sports serve as a training ground for communicating, learning from, and working with others. Watching your child develop strong, positive friendships is the hidden treasure in youth sports. Spending time working and learning together helps strengthen these friendships and fosters positive, balanced relationships. Sports bring people with shared interests together, promoting communication and friendship. Young athletes will laugh, sweat, and cry with their teammates. Good teammates push each other to improve and support one another when needed. Always remember that making friends is one of the main reasons we started all this, and even having just one best friend is worth it.

Teamwork is an attribute that you should look for in the club, the coach, and every adult involved with the team, including parents. Teaching kids to work together must be supported at every level of your sport. Most sports involve a sports club, a team, coaches, and, finally, the players. The coach is at the forefront of encouraging trust, camaraderie, and teamwork amongst their players. How they bring in new players will show you everything you need to know. Do they bring the player in and instantly make them a member of the team, or do they throw them in to sink or swim? If a coach doesn't understand how it feels for a player to join a new team full of strangers, then it is a red flag for me.

When it comes to teamwork and building strong relationships, coaches cannot do it alone. Teamwork is inclusive, involving every member of the program. First, ensure that the club your team belongs to is family-oriented, works closely with families, and genuinely cares about its players. Second, observe the parents on the sidelines during games. Look for a supportive atmosphere with people who positively uplift the team, as this encourages teamwork. Avoid teams with adults who are negative or overreact, as such behavior is not conducive to cooperation and teamwork.

The best teams are just groups of friends playing together and having fun. Teamwork helps everyone feel included and comfortable. Struggling and losing don't feel so bad with a friend, and winning is much better when you can celebrate with someone. Making friends and learning to work with others provide essential benefits for children.

Social interaction has always been crucial for kids. Parents should regularly encourage social activities, such as playdates, sports, academic groups, and other enjoyable pursuits. Isolation can slow emotional and cognitive growth. If you see a child who seems to stay on the fringes of a team or doesn't fit in, it's helpful to encourage other children to make an effort to include them. Many kids are shy and afraid of new people and settings, which is entirely understandable. Sports settings can feel like being on a stage in front of all the spectators. Most shy children are insecure and can emerge from their shell in a safe sporting environment with parental support.

If a team has players being excluded or bullied, this is not a healthy team environment. This kind of behavior is a bad sign. Good coaches will not tolerate their teams excluding or bullying other players. Sports are about inclusion, not exclusion. Sportsmanship, fair play, teamwork—everything that sports stand for—is against bullying and exclusion. All my players were treated with respect, and they were expected to reciprocate that courtesy to everyone.

5. Everyone involved should act with good sportsmanship

Games are only a small part of the sports experience. Being a good sport is a quality that manifests at every practice and in our personal lives. It means not embarrassing opponents. It means helping them up after they fall. Good sportsmanship is not running up scores on teams. It's treating others fairly and with kindness. Good sportsmanship is learning to empathize with your fellow humans, even if they are your opponents. Players, coaches, and teams will show you who they are by how they treat their opponents.

In life, we all experience both wins and losses in various ways. Learning to lose gracefully and respectfully is a necessary life skill. Sports are a great way to show kids that life won't always go their way, but they can handle it. The world will not collapse if they lose a few games. They will succeed by getting up and trying again. This is an area where the coach and parents should lead by example. No adult should put so much emphasis on winning that losing becomes unacceptable. There is much to be learned from a loss.

Over the years, I have seen parents of talented players move their kids from one team to another and frequently switch coaches. The main reason is that they want a team that looks good to the parents. They often say it's about the player, but usually it's about the parent. If you start picking a team based on scores and records, you're going the wrong way. Anyone with basic knowledge can gather good players and win games, but you want something more. You're looking for a positive experience for your whole family, and finding the right team is a key part of that.

The right team environment is important because you'll spend a lot of time with team-mates and their families. If you look for re-spect, self-discipline, good work ethic, team-work and good sportsmanship, you will make the right choice. Ultimately, finding the right team is essential, and the team's skipper is al-ways the coach.

Finding the Right Coach

Parents should carefully research coaches before selecting a team. It's a mistake to choose a team simply because they are in a higher division or have a winning record. Many promising young athletes have moved to higher-division teams only to realize it was a step down in key areas, such as coaching and the team environment.

Selecting the right coach is one of the most important decisions you can make. The coach sets the tone and priorities for the team. You need someone trustworthy who can effectively teach your child. You want a coach who shares your morals and core values. Since they will be working with your child, you need a level-headed, fair, and honest coach who communicates well with both parents and children.

Five Qualities of a Good Coach

1. Good coaches are fun!

A coach needs to be fun and be able to entertain kids. I don't mean that we need a clown out there, but learning a sport involves a lot of repetition. Getting kids to do the same thing repeatedly only works if the coach can keep them engaged and having fun. Always look for a coach who smiles. This is kids' sports, and we don't want a coach who takes it too seriously. Being too serious takes away the fun for everyone involved. There will be times when the players need a coach who can make them laugh.

I recall losing a State Cup game badly, and my players were pretty upset The parents came over slowly with sad faces and boxes of doughnuts. After my post-game speech, I could see that many players still looked pretty down, so I jokingly mashed a doughnut on top of one of my players' heads. Of course, this led to me being attacked by a team of screaming kids wielding doughnuts like clubs!

Years later, no one remembered the score of that game, but we all still remember the Great Doughnut Battle of 2001! Coaches who laugh and can entertain make the experience enjoyable for everyone.

2. Good coaches are honest and respectful

Coaches should be truthful and respectful. Every parent I know wants to raise an honest, respectful child. To do that, we need to show them what respectful adults look like, even in challenging situations. If you see a coach disrespecting a child or someone else in front of a child, find a different coach. Children learn by observing how adults behave.

I ran indoor sports leagues for years, and it was outrageous how much effort we had to put into stopping coaches from cheating. Cheating in youth sports is out of hand. We had a list of teams and a few entire academies whose games were monitored by staff to stop directors and coaches from sneaking overage players into youth indoor winter league games. This is a deal breaker for me.

Adults must take responsibility for raising our children. If you participate on a team with a coach who cheats or disrespects others, you are sending your child the message that such behavior is acceptable. This is unacceptable, and it's precisely what we want to avoid. It can be something as simple as using an overage player or bringing in stronger guest players to win games; the message remains the same.

Cheating is never okay. Don't support bad coaches and programs; keep your child away from dishonest and disrespectful people.

3. Good coaches are teachers

Coaches should understand the game and be able to teach it. Knowing how to play a sport does not automatically qualify someone to teach it. To be an effective coach, one must study the game and develop a deeper understanding of it. Coaches should continually educate themselves on rule changes and new teaching techniques and philosophies. You want a coach who knows that youth sports is about more than wins and losses.

Knowing and understanding are only part of the deal. Coaches need to break down and explain concepts clearly so that children can learn them effectively. Kids need to be told, shown, and then allowed to practice the skills. Coaches should be educated, intelligent, and able to simplify the game for kids. Teaching a group of children isn't easy, and a coach should never try to teach something that they don't know or understand. Nothing will damage a coach's credibility faster than teaching a player something that is incorrect.

4. Good coaches are motivators

A coach should be able to motivate players when they need it. Think about how many great speeches you've heard from famous coaches. Knute Rockne, Vince Lombardi, John Wooden, and Jimmy V. were incredible motivators who lifted their teams to championships. The coach is the team leader, and leaders can help players reach their full potential. There will be times when teams and players need their coach to lift them with their words. A great coach must be able to inspire their team and players to strive for greater effort and improvement. Coaches who can motivate their players are powerful coaches.

There are many ways to motivate people. Good coaches do not need to use fear or intimidation to pressure players into working hard. It is not a coach's job to scare or humiliate kids; nor should they rely on peer pressure to motivate players. These tactics often tear a team apart. Players and coaches should always be positive and supportive. Good coaches motivate kids by making the game fun and challenging. Great coaches make it so enjoyable and teach kids so well that their players want to try new things and excel!

Great coaches are rare, but many good people out there give it their best. Find someone who is dedicated and genuinely cares about the kids. This applies to any coach, whether it is a volunteer parent or a paid professional. If the coach does not care equally about every child, they are not worth the time or money invested in them.

5. Good coaches care about each player's development

One of the more important qualities to look for in a coach is how they handle player development/progress. Good coaches challenge their top players while ensuring that every player can keep up. Coaches who leave kids behind should, in turn, be left behind, because you want a coach who can effectively teach all kids. Anyone can put eleven kids on a field and call themselves a coach. Great coaches are teachers who don't kick kids out of class when they're falling behind; they find a better way to teach them.

Evaluating Coaches and Teams

When evaluating coaches and considering teams, several key indicators can give valuable insights. Remember what we said at the start of this book: sports can bring out the worst in people. We can all sit in a team meeting or practice and be the perfect sports parent or coach. Things change when we are on the sidelines of competitive games. That's when character is tested, and discipline is essential. Before joining any team, go watch a game. Observe how the players, coach, and parents behave during games. That will reveal what you need to know.

The head coach is the leader of their team. Good leaders prioritize their players' well-being and position them in the best possible way to succeed. Coaches can make or break their teams. It is the coach who sets the tone and creates the team environment. Please note that each coach may define success differently; therefore, consider the following key factors when evaluating a coach and their team.

Meet with Potential Coaches

Coaches should be prepared to provide parents with basic information, including their team's priorities, coaching philosophy, playing strategy, and team goals. We want to ensure that the coach's priorities align with yours and that they possess the necessary skills, temperament, and ability to teach your child effectively.

Generally, parents should meet regularly with anyone who will be working with their child. It's beneficial to spend a few minutes getting to know the person in a position of trust with your kid. Feel free to ask them questions about playing time, player expectations, and their aspirations for their players. When talking to a coach, trust your instincts. If you don't feel comfortable talking to them, they might not be the right coach for you. If having fun isn't a priority, or if the coach seems more focused on their record than on their players, I recommend finding a different coach.

Ask About Player Retention

Nothing reveals more about a coach than how many players leave their team each season. A good coach develops players and keeps the team together. A coach who keeps players happy and helps them improve is a teacher. "Poachers" or "recruiting coaches" are coaches who focus more on recruiting great players than on developing them. These coaches should be avoided because they do not teach; they gather good players trained by others. They prioritize winning over development, which is not beneficial for your child because it harms their development. These coaches run their teams like treadmills, dumping players as quickly as they can be replaced. To be a good coach, they must develop and retain their players.

Watch the Coach, Coach

Parents should never assume a coach is good just because they have a winning record, play in a high division, or have a sports background. It's important to observe how they coach. This will give you valuable insight into their character and mindset. How do they run practice? Are their players having fun? Do they genuinely care? Go and watch a game. Do they allow their players to play freely, or are they constantly yelling at them? Do they show respect to referees and opposing coaches? Do they teach during games? Are they having fun? Don't hesitate to talk to other parents on the sidelines about potential coaches. You want to ensure their behavior aligns with the role model you want your child to emulate.

Research the Club or Academy

Academies and clubs vary significantly in size and structure. Some are as small as a few teams, while larger clubs can have many more. Some are highly organized, while others are just collections of teams. Ask around to learn about the club's or academy's reputation. Larger clubs with more teams can help ensure players stay at developmentally appropriate levels, which is always best for the player. A bigger, more organized club may offer more benefits than a smaller one, such as position-specific trainers or extra support staff. However, if your child is not interested in a more competitive environment, small clubs may be the right fit. It's essential to do your due diligence.

Summary

Once you find the right club, level of play,

coach, and team, stay alert. Coaches are human and can lose their way. I recommend speaking with the coach monthly to check on your child's progress, ensure the coach is well, and stay informed about any team issues. Go and watch practices regularly to see how the kids are treating each other. Teams can develop problems that hinder their players' and the team's growth and enjoyment. Kids can split into little "groups" that cause drama. Parent groups can form and break teams from within through petty jealousies and disputes. If you keep your priorities straight, you can find the right environment and protect your family from these issues.

Understanding
Player Development

I write this section cautiously because I do not wish to pigeonhole any coaches or players. While every player is different, there are some basic skill packages and milestones that you can look for as your young player grows. The information in this section is intended to provide parents with a roadmap for a player's development. This knowledge can help you manage your expectations and standards by providing you with road signs to follow as your player grows into the sport. However, it must be noted that while the parents can see the map, the coaches are driving. Parents can outline a series of progressive steps, but when and how quickly players climb them can vary greatly.

Progression is the basic human desire to improve and face new challenges as we learn new skills. Kids are little humans, and humans are natural learners. As learners, we want to improve as we learn a new skill. Children are always learning, and they will want to improve as they participate in sports. Players will want to progress in every aspect of their sport, including fitness, skills, and understanding of the game. This desire for progress is what drives player development. It's essential to recognize that children will lose interest in any activity if they become stuck at a particular level. Let's be honest: we all lose interest if we can't progress. Progression is a vital part of youth sports that is often overlooked or mishandled. It is essential and something that every player, coach, and parent will naturally expect.

For player retention, coaches must consistently challenge stronger players while ensuring that all players can keep up. If training is too easy, stronger players will become bored and want to quit. If training is too challenging, players who struggle to keep up may become unhappy and want to quit. Teammates can increase the pressure for progress through their level of play, encouraging others to work harder to stay competitive. This is where individual responsibility starts to emerge. Kids learn at different speeds, and as they discover their abilities, they'll recognize when they need to put in extra effort. Responsible players will make that choice on their own, but guidance along the way is always helpful. Factors such as fitness, interest, personal issues, and confidence can impact progress. That's why it's so important to allow players to set their own pace of development.

Proper progression for players or an entire team of kids is complex, but when managed well, it is achievable. In youth sports, it is essential to allow players to develop at their own pace. A player's progress will be judged by their coaches, teammates, spectators, and themselves. Your child will need to learn how to manage all that feedback, and they will need parental help to do it. Players who learn to set their own standards for progress will be able to evaluate themselves fairly and stay protected from criticism.

Player development refers to an athlete's overall progress as a player. Players will always want to improve in every aspect of the game, but they will not always progress all the time. Sports involve so many elements that it is difficult to improve at everything all the time. Players will work to improve their fitness, skill, intelligence, decision-making, speed of play, and communication skills. Depending on how those things develop, secondary but equally vital skills will also grow, such as confidence, experience, and instincts.

I have seen many graphs showing expected player development, and I've always disliked them because they try to put players into boxes, which ignores the fact that kids are all different. No two players will develop the same way. Each person will have their bursts of growth and times that seem like lulls. Just like with growth spurts, everyone is different, and each scenario is unique. I've had players who peaked at twelve, and I once had a girl who became a phenomenal player at sixteen. I've seen many players with good size or speed fall short because they relied too much on their physical abilities. At the same time, I coached a girl named Melissa, the most petite girl on every team we played, yet no one could take the ball from her. Her balance and skill were exceptional from a young age, and she continued to develop them, winning several State Championships. The point is that every player and family takes their own path. How your player develops depends a lot on how much they want to improve. Still, I understand that it can be helpful for parents to have some idea or roadmap for how players are likely to progress in their sport.

The following stages of development were

developed for soccer, but I am confident that they apply to any youth sport. However, it is a guide that uses age as the primary variable. Many kids start sports later than others, and parents worry they will be too far behind and unable to catch up. The good news is that as children grow older, they tend to learn more quickly. Late starters can catch up if they genuinely want to. If your child begins late, ignore the age guidelines and use this as a guide to watch their progress through the stages.

Stage I : Ages 6-9

At this young age, everything centers around having fun and developing basic skills. Players need to learn essential technical fundamentals, such as touching the ball, dribbling, passing, receiving, and shooting. Since this age group has a lot to learn and everything will be new to them, their playing positions should change often. Kids learn in different ways, so any new skill should be explained, demonstrated, and then practiced. The primary focus at younger ages is on technical growth. Kids are learning machines, and they'll pick up both good and bad habits.

These early ages are perfect for instilling good habits. Players should understand that sports are a privilege earned through dedication and effort. Good behavior at home, good grades in school, and solid practice routines should all be required to earn the right to play in games. Kids shouldn't regularly leave games or practices feeling disappointed, guilty, or anxious. These are early indications of a problem and clear signs that a child is not having the fun experience they deserve.

Parents with children at this stage can start setting boundaries regarding how much their child can invest in their sport and begin setting realistic expectations. Always remember that kids are meant to make mistakes. These young players will make many of them. No one should ever yell at them or punish them for making mistakes. The more mistakes they make, the more they learn.

Stage II : Ages 10-14

This middle group will refine their technical skills through dedication and repeated practice. These players will have developed or will soon develop the skills needed to be effective on the field. During this phase, they will learn more advanced techniques such as defending, field vision, and decision-making. Players will build further confidence in their basic skills, including dribbling, passing, receiving, and shooting. Their specific skill set will start to become evident during this stage. Some players will develop physical attributes that enhance their abilities, such as height, strength, or speed. Others may excel in more talent-based areas, such as field vision, decision-making, or goal scoring. Ultimately, a player's skill set will influence where and how they play on the field. This is when player positions are solidified. As a coach, I can tell you that it doesn't matter what position you want them to play; the player's skill set will eventually determine where they should play. Some players are natural defenders and dislike letting opponents get past them. Others have incredible dribbling skills and are offensively minded. It all depends on the player.

Coaches will introduce team tactical training, including formations, defensive strategies, and attacking tactics. This stage will blend technical and tactical training, depending on the team's skill level, and will become increasingly mental over time. All these topics should be covered at the coach's discretion. This is not an adult professional league like the NFL or NHL, where coaches are paid to develop a system and recruit professional players to fit it. In youth sports, you play the hand you're dealt. If you don't get superstar players at every position, which you won't, then you need to work with the players you have on your roster. Never forget that every team and every player develops at their own pace. Every coach should know that and expect to adjust their play strategy to allow for player growth and development.

It is a disheartening fact that according to the National Alliance for Youth Sports, 70 percent of children quit competitive sports by the age of thirteen. The most common reasons are excessive pressure and the fact that it is no longer enjoyable.

Stage III : Ages 15-17

This final stage will move further away from technical training and focus more on tactical play. Tactical training teaches players how, where, and when to move on the field, helping them understand their teammates' actions during games and fostering teamwork. At this point, players will continue to practice their technical skills to stay sharp, while coaches focus on maximizing the overall team performance. Teenage players and their coaches aim to compete and enjoy the experience, but losing isn't fun, so competition can get intense. During their teenage years, players need parental guidance as they undergo many physical and emotional changes. Sports serve as a great outlet, but emotions can become overwhelming without proper management. This is where your parental guidance becomes essential.

Fifteen-year-old Russell was an exceptional soccer player. He was tall and lean, built like a sprinter, and had the speed and shot to be outstanding. Russell had all the qualities to be a great player, but at fifteen, he was an insecure kid who had recently lost his father. After his personal loss, he threw himself into soccer and was never content with his performance. Russell had developed unreasonable expectations and took the game too seriously. He was upset after every game and practice, always wanting more. He would lose his temper on the field and be very hard on himself. It was evident that he wasn't enjoying himself.

Russell's mother and I struggled to help him set reasonable expectations for his performance and winning. I often had to sit with him and help him regain control of his emotions when he became emotionally overwhelmed. I patiently showed him how his feelings and overinvestment were creating unnecessary pressure and damaging his performance. It took time, but eventually we worked together to establish limits on the emotional energy he would devote to the game. Russell was one of the lucky ones who found balance, and he carried that skill into adulthood, including as a professional soccer player for a short time in Germany. I felt fortunate to have worked with him, and he remains a friend to this day.

At every stage of development, it is the coach's responsibility to adapt to the players' and the team's needs. Every player's and every team's level of progression will differ slightly depending on the coach and the player's abilities, which is why choosing the right coach is essential. You want a coach you can trust to prioritize your child's development, while also giving equal attention to each player and the whole team. Player development falls squarely within the coach's purview. Parents must take a back seat and allow the coach to do their job. However, they should be able to track team and player progression.

Some teams progress more slowly or quickly than others. Some players start playing sports later or develop their skills later than others. Players and teams can gain ground because older players tend to be more mature, smarter, and better at learning. It is the coach's job to assess and train players appropriately, and it is the players' responsibility to work hard and stay focused. A great coach and a group of dedicated, hard-working players can become a dream team!

Tryouts

If your child is trying out for a team, remember to approach tryouts with empathy. Trying to make a team can be very stressful if parents don't handle it properly. Imagine the courage it takes for a child to walk into a group of kids and perform. Kids don't like being singled out, and they definitely don't like not getting what they want. We need to be careful about this. We want to prevent any child from feeling like they aren't good enough, because that feeling can last a long time.

Parents must do their due diligence when choosing a team. You should visit the coach and meet them. If your child is a novice, consider trying out for a team where they have a good chance of making it. You have nothing to prove by your child making a particular team. A youth sports team isn't a badge of honor or a bragging point. More importantly, not making a team can make your child dislike sports. Far too many parents fall into the trap of believing that higher-ranked teams confer prestige upon them or the players. Youth sports are about the Three F's: Fun, Friends, and Fitness, not prestige.

If your child is moving up to a higher level of competition, you need to prepare both your child and yourself properly. The first thing you should do is explain to your child that making a team isn't just about being good enough. Sometimes it's about being the player that the team needs. This means that your player must fill a specific role or contribute to the roster. It also means that players must have a successful tryout and be someone the coaches believe will fit into their team. Coaches are generally cautious with their teams, and they should be loyal to their players. For a player to get onto a higher-level team, they don't just have to be good enough—they also may need to be significantly better than someone already on the team.

Before any tryouts, parents and their players should scout the team, speak with the coach, and watch a few games. Use all the parameters listed above to judge potential teams. This gives you the best chance of making the squad and ensuring it is the right team for you. You must let your child know that if they don't make the team, there could be many reasons other than that they aren't good enough. We don't want to set our kids up for failure.

Summary

Understanding your player's natural progression helps you avoid many problems young players often encounter in youth sports. Parents must stay grounded and help manage their child's investment in sports. Allowing players to progress and develop at their own pace ensures that we don't add unnecessary pressure to the game. Let players choose how much they want to invest in their sport and what they expect to gain in return. Some will want to win championships, while others will simply want to hang out with friends and enjoy the game. Parents should walk alongside their player and ensure they stay within appropriate boundaries and stay on course. Kids tend to wander from the path, and parents serve as the guardrails.

Supporting Youth Sports

If appropriately managed, youth sports will give your family more than it takes. Your kids will make friends and, in turn, you will meet new friends who have children similar in age to your own, which is always lovely. Your other kids will meet the other siblings on the team. As a family, your network will grow, and many opportunities may come from those relationships. You might meet a family that loves camping like yours or other parents who share your passion for music. You may find other parents who are willing to babysit for you. I once met a great parent who ended up collaborating with me on editing this book. You never know what youth sports might hold for you and your family.

As good parents and people, we all know we want to support our children. When getting involved in youth sports, it's essential to recognize that your support is what keeps youth sports thriving; parents like you who get off work and hustle to get your kids to practice; parents who make time to watch practices so their kids know they are interested in their lives—moms and dads who lug team tents and equipment to games. You all make it happen, but you are not the only ones. Your child is your world, but when you get into youth sports, every child out there is someone's world.

We must all recognize that while your child is your primary concern, they cannot be your only concern. We are responsible for all the kids out there. Whenever you see a child in need, you should lend a helping hand. In youth sports, every kid could use your support as they strive to do their best, regardless of the level of play. If this is your first time being involved in youth sports, let's ensure we are all on the same page. As a parent or an adult involved in an activity that involves kids, you have a responsibility to every child out there. Sports are never about one kid, one team, or one game. Sports bring people together for the benefit of children. Keeping that in mind will help you stay grounded.

I watched a video the other day where a youth game of American football erupted into chaos after a child was knocked unconscious by a block. While the child lay on the ground, grown adults celebrated over him. Coaches and parents started fighting everywhere as a single coach bent over the fallen child. What kind of person celebrates when a child gets hurt?

Supporting Officials

Youth sporting events are fantastic for kids, and without officials, there would be no games. Referees and game officials are human, and in fact, many of them are also kids. They will do their best to perform their duties, but they will make mistakes and occasionally make biased decisions. If you accept this truth now, you might not become so outraged when it happens.

One issue with youth sports is that people often confuse them with professional sports. Adults at professional sporting events frequently insult and abuse referees and players. Anyone who has played in front of a crowd and endured fans' abuse can confirm that it can turn a dream into a nightmare. In a professional environment, many adults believe that because they bought a ticket, and the referees are grown-ups and professionals earning a lot of money, they should be able to handle the abuse. We have spent generations dehumanizing officials, and the consequences are troubling. Few jobs even come close to the level of abuse referees endure. The threats and abuse faced by referees are unacceptable, yet many fans and parents have become numb to them.

What most fans fail to recognize is that their negativity bias causes them to remember the referee's bad call over the hundreds of good ones. Negativity bias is the tendency to focus more on adverse events than on positive ones. It's a fundamental characteristic of humans to notice and remember the negative because that's where our attention tends to go. So, we recall mistakes more often than we recall correct calls. However, we must acknowledge that in any job, a person who makes one mistake out of every hundred decisions would be considered exemplary. Yet, as a teenage referee, your safety might be at risk when working a Sunday morning peewee football game if you make a mistake.

Kids' sports are different. You didn't pay money for a ticket, and everyone out there is a kid. No one, not even referees at professional sports games, deserves to be abused at their jobs. It's even worse when it happens to young referees. And the absolute truth is that yelling and insulting referees or officials accomplishes nothing. In all my years of playing and coaching soccer, I have never seen a parent, coach, or spectator change a referee's mind by yelling at them. Usually, it's the opposite, so if you ever find yourself talking to a referee, recognize that you're the problem. A referee has a tough job. They must make split-second decisions in a fast-paced sport involving kids. It's a lot of responsibility, and it should be a respected job. We wouldn't have youth sports without them. Referees can choose from any number of jobs, but they come out and face abuse so that our kids can play a game. Everyone who decides to invest their time in youth sports is a gift to us all. No one should criticize referees or any game officials.

Parents should avoid speaking to the referee or other players on the field unless they choose to throw a thank you their way. This is about a kids' game, and the truth is that words can cause a lot of harm, so be careful with yours.

Supporting Coaches

Your relationship with your child's coach is essential. A good coach is another adult teacher who can reinforce important lessons and serve as a good role model for your child. All good teachers are a gift to our community and should be respected and admired. You should feel comfortable speaking with your child's coach. Whenever you approach a coach, remember that they are trying to help your child.

Coaches are good people trying to pass on their knowledge to kids. It is a wonderful endeavor, but all coaches know that every season they will take their share of lumps. They will lose games and make mistakes, and they will also be criticized, second-guessed, and sometimes insulted by other teams and players, but mainly by the parents of their own team. Coaches are on your side, but sadly, due to a few problem parents, it can be hard for coaches to believe parents are on their side.

When thinking of your coach, show empathy for someone who is constantly under scrutiny and surrounded by critics who, unfortunately, have no problem second-guessing them right to their face. Coaches are more committed to the team's success than anyone else. It is their job, and they will gauge their success by how well their teams perform. No one wants to be bad at their job.

Once, a father told me I didn't understand what the "wingback" position was in soccer. He had played in college and didn't want his son to play like a wingback. Instead, he preferred his son at right midfield. For those unfamiliar, a wing-back plays just behind the midfielder and often runs past them. During a game, the positions interchange so frequently that his son was sometimes in the right midfield, but this wasn't good enough for him. His son fit the position I had him playing, yet this father had no hesitation in telling me I was wrong and that I didn't know what I was talking about. I recall him offering to take me out for a beer to educate me about the wingback position. I declined his offer.

This kind of situation often happens to coaches. When you tell a coach how to do their job, you are belittling them. Parents are their children's protectors, but coaches must be allowed to coach. If you have an issue with a decision your coach made, you can discuss it with them, but you should approach the conversation with the right attitude.

You should develop a solid relationship with the person coaching your child. A coach can be one of the most important people in your child's life. You should know them, and they should know you. You should feel free to ask how they are doing, how they think the team is performing, or even what they see as their primary concerns for the team. Just be sure to ask for their opinion, not give yours. A good coach will reach out if they are concerned about your child or need your thoughts on a new approach with your child. Every coach I know is willing to speak with parents, but they do not appreciate being second-guessed, ganged up on, or interrogated.

Early in my career, a group of parents gathered and confronted me after a game. They didn't understand my kickoff strategy and were upset that I wasn't listening to their concerns. The truth was, I had heard their concerns but still chose not to change my approach. My strategy was simple: keep possession, play the ball backward when necessary, and try to move forward as a team. The parents wanted me to adjust my strategy to their preferences, and despite my repeated explanation, they resisted. They were second-guessing me. Mind you, none of these parents had ever coached soccer. They saw us playing the ball backward on kick-offs and then losing possession in our own half. The obvious, faster fix was to boot the ball into the opposing half, giving the opponents the ball and putting us on defense. They wanted me to tell the kids to kick the ball deep into the attacking end and go get it, but that wasn't the possession style of play I wanted for the team.

The subject was brought up again at the next parent meeting. It was here that a new parent—who later became a close friend—rose to ask for everyone's attention. He smiled and said,

"My name is Steve, and I know I'm new to the team, but I am surprised by this discussion. Pete was hired to coach this team, and now everyone here is telling him how to do his job. I cannot imagine operating on a patient and Pete walking into the room to tell me where to cut." Many parents found it hilarious, while those who had been questioning me sheepishly settled into their seats. I explained that if they were patient, my plan would work as the players' skills improved— and it did. It turned out Steve was a world-renowned cancer surgeon, but I didn't find out until years later.

Parents who constantly question the coach's decisions about player positions, playing time, and strategies undermine their coach. Parents should feel comfortable speaking with their coach, but they must accept the coach's decisions and opinions; otherwise, they should consider finding another coach. You don't want to be the reason your child is removed from a team. Coaches are human, and a kid whose parent is difficult and constantly undermines the coach is more likely to be removed from the team roster. Coaches will protect their teams, and problem parents wreck many of them. Parents can always ask the coach what their child needs to do to improve, but before asking the coach, it's better to ask their child first. Players should already know what the coach has instructed them to work on.

We must remember that coaches and league officials are people, just like you and me. Often, they volunteer to be a coach or official, and they deserve our respect and appreciation. I do not believe people get involved in youth sports to hurt kids. One of the reasons they do it is because it's fun, and for them, being around kids is a joy. If you have done your research and carefully chosen your coach, let them do their job. When attending games, be prepared to treat all coaches, officials, and parents with respect. Most of them are good people, so be supportive and positive, and everything will be fine.

Playing Time

Any parent who complains to the coach about playing time may unintentionally cause more problems. Questioning a coach's decisions is normal, but that doesn't mean it should be acceptable. Coaching is a tough job that requires patience and effort. When you start pressuring a coach to give your child more playing time, you're treading on dangerous ground. First, you risk damaging your relationship with the coach. Imagine if your coach came into your workplace and tried to tell you how to do your job—that would seem outrageous. Second, you could be undermining your child's efforts. What if you complain and then your child gets more playing time? Was it because they earned it, or to get you off the coach's back? Your child might wonder.

Whenever a parent approached me about their child needing more playing time, which happened quite often, the first question I asked was, "Have you spoken with your child?" I asked this question for two reasons. First, I wanted to determine whether the player or the parent was unhappy. More often than not, the players were fine, while the parents wanted more. Second, I wanted to see if the player knew what they needed to do to increase their playing time. Players who really wanted to play more would always know the answer to the question. It's what they would have been working on in practice. If a player didn't know the answer, then either the coach didn't tell them, or the player didn't really care about more playing time. If the parent had not spoken with their child before asking me, then I would usually bring the player over and ask them to answer the question. In the rare instance the player couldn't answer the question, I would do it for them.

If you have a decent, honest coach, then they are trying to be fair to their players and win games. Your player isn't playing more because they aren't good enough to take the minutes from the other players. Coaches can give you many reasons, but the truth is that the better players give teams a better chance of winning. Coaches are not out there to lose, so it is in their best interests to play the best team. It really is that simple, but it's also not the end of the world. Your child will not be the best at everything they do, and that should be okay.

You need to be able to trust that your coach has your child's best interests in mind at all times. There is nothing wrong with discussing your child's abilities and how they affect their playing time with a coach, but never try to lobby a coach for more playing time. If your child is unhappy with their playing time and has a good coach, then they should know what they need to do to improve. If you ever have reason to believe that your child isn't playing for any reason other than their ability, then you should address it and find another team.

24-Hour Rule

Generally, it's best not to speak with coaches for 24 hours after a game. After a game, coaches are usually busy with players and processing what happened. Coaches are human and very invested in their teams. Losing games or performing poorly can be upsetting for everyone. It's always better to let cooler heads prevail and give coaches some space after games.

A good friend of mine shared a story about how a parent was ready to fight him after a game for not playing his daughter in the second half. Since the parent had approached the coach before speaking to his child, he felt pretty foolish when he found out that his daughter had refused to play because of a sour stomach. The coach turned and walked away from the confrontation to avoid setting a bad example for his players, and the parent sent an apology letter that night.

It's usually better to keep a cool head, as the parent-coach relationship is vital to the player's success. It's a good idea to schedule a time to talk with your coach. Keep it friendly and respectful, and your coach should have no problem talking with you. When speaking with a coach, remember to start with questions, trust their answers, have an open mind, and always talk with your child first. Coaches should be more than happy to speak with you about your child. It's part of the job.

Cheering

On game day, kids will get excited because you are coming to watch them play. They will want everyone to share their enthusiasm, and while cheering is important, self-control is even more so. Yelling and cheering for your child's team is fun, but it's essential to recognize that when one competitor succeeds, the other faces disappointment. I've seen some parents who want to be the loudest in the stands, laughing and celebrating their team's successes. They draw a lot of attention and claim it's for their kid, but in truth, they are the only ones enjoying the attention. This is about more than just your child. Good sportsmanship means not rubbing it in on the opposing children.

Adults should never use cheering to manipulate a game or to insult children. I have heard this many times from coaches and parents. Coaches and parents often yell things like, "You can beat him; he's not as fast as you," or "Take the ball from her. You are so much better than her." Parents often criticize goalies for making mistakes, "The keeper is shaky, keep shooting." This isn't cheering. It is an attempt to manipulate a game by undermining a young person's confidence. It is the worst kind of behavior from an adult and has no place in youth sports.

I have a friend named Johanna who told me a story about a time she was playing in a tournament when she missed a penalty shot in the first game. Her team ended up playing the same team in a semi-final a couple of days later. During that game, another penalty opportunity arose, and Jo's coach wanted her to take it. She was their best player, and her coach wanted her to overcome the memory of her miss. Just before she struck the ball, one of the parents on the other team yelled, "She missed the last one, so be ready when she misses this one!" I called Johanna's father after hearing this story and asked him about it. He didn't remember how the tournament went, but he remembered the person yelling that about his child. Johanna scored the penalty, but the damage was done.

Good parenting involves understanding that there's a right way and a wrong way to cheer for kids' sports. Remember to support all the kids out there; they all deserve it. Clapping and cheering are important, and our kids will expect us to do it. Just remember that kids don't like being called out in front of people, so being the loudest isn't the best way to support them. You help and support all the kids out there by respecting their feelings and demonstrating how adults should behave towards all the children on both teams.

I have always encouraged parents to cheer for their kids and give positive feedback. Players will make mistakes and have bad games. They will stumble and fall, but the most important thing is that they are trying, and that should always be rewarded. Mistakes happen in split seconds and are often irreversible, while these young athletes give it their all at every practice and every game. All the kids' efforts must be prioritized, recognized, and appreciated. Remember, this isn't pro sports. These athletes are all kids, and they are all trying their best. If you applaud their effort, you may find yourself applauding for both teams. Would that be so terrible?

Summary

At this point, it needs to be stated that in sports, there will be trash talk, your child will be fouled, and they might face dirty play. There are inherent risks in sports, and it's essential to prepare for them. Everything we do carries some level of risk. Athletes get injured sometimes. You can't just yell your way into getting everyone else to protect your child. It would be great if coaches, other players, or referees helped, but yelling at them won't make it happen. As a parent, deciding whether to allow your child to participate is your responsibility. It is also your responsibility to support all the people involved in making youth sports available. Officials, coaches, parents, and players deserve our respect and appreciation. Let's give it to them.

What the Kids
See and Hear

Congratulations on being a good parent. Parenting is both the hardest and the most rewarding thing you'll ever do. Anyone willing to keep learning for their children's benefit is a good parent. Showing up is the most critical part of parenting, and you're doing just that by reading this book. Thank you, and I hope I've helped you in your journey. This chapter is close to my heart.

It's insightful to know what coaches see in the kids when parents coach from the sidelines, cheer like fanatics, or call out coaches and officials. Most of the time, when adults misbehave on the sidelines, their kids are on the other side of the field paying the price. Out-of-control parents embarrass their kids, and children can relentlessly tease one another. An out-of-control or embarrassing parent opens their child up to endless ridicule. Virtually every time a parent managed to get my attention during a game, their kid was humiliated on the field. I recall a few times when the referee asked me to walk across the field and ask parents to settle down. Can you imagine my displeasure at having to leave my team of kids to walk across a soccer field and ask a bunch of adults to behave themselves? It is neither the coach's job nor should it be to protect their players from embarrassing or harmful adult behavior.

As we grow into adulthood, we often forget the good and innocent things about being a child. The world makes us more goal-oriented, more direct. We learn how to adapt or hide our insecurities. Far too often, we lose the fun of things by making them too serious. I saw parents doing things that embarrassed and/or confused their child without taking the time to consider how their child might feel. You must imagine how your child might feel watching their parents scream at a referee in front of everyone over a missed call. Even if the parent is right, it isn't respectful. Are they really doing that for their kid?

Most children are naïve, emotional, intelligent, dependent, and above all, insecure. They have little control over their lives and rely entirely on their parents. They lack the knowledge or experience required to be strong, independent people. It is the parent's job to prepare them for life and help them become confident, independent adults. Of course, there are kids out there who seem to contradict this idea, but most of those children are just pretending. A word or two from their parents or coach can bring the entire façade down.

Kids don't realize it, but they hold a lot of fear. They are scared to stand out. They are afraid of being left behind. They are fearful of embarrassment and ridicule. They are worried they might let their parents down. This is why kids cling tightly to their parents. They stay close to them to feel safe. Parents should be a place of safety and comfort, not a source of embarrassment, shame, or ridicule.

Most bad adult behavior affects the players in one of three ways. Mainly, it embarrasses them, which turns a fun game into a bad experience. Second, it takes their focus from their sport and puts it on their parent. And third, it hurts their confidence on the team. As stated, kids are not strong, confident adults. They are insecure, and their parents' acting up is embarrassing. Most people prefer to avoid the spotlight rather than dance in it.

One of the most common instances of adult misbehavior is when parents scream and yell or lose their composure when their child scores. First, this takes attention away from the players and puts it squarely on the parent. Please don't be that parent. Second, as mentioned, over-celebration is poor sportsmanship, and your kids will look to you for this lesson. By overdoing it, you are embarrassing yourself, your team, the other team, and your child. It is reasonable to be happy when your team succeeds, but you should also be aware that there are other kids out there and that their parents are sitting next to you.

Another widespread mistake is parents coaching their kids from the sidelines during games and matches. Regardless of the sport, players have a coach whom they respect. A parent on the sidelines trying to do the coach's job is a bad look. First, it distracts a child from making their own decisions. From birth, they have been trained to listen to their parent's voice. Now they are playing a sport, and they can't think because all they hear is their parent telling them what to do. Second, this hurts the players' confidence and embarrasses them. They will wonder why their parents don't believe they can do it themselves. Athletes need confidence to perform well, and constant direction can tie up their most crucial asset: their brains.

Next on our list of common problems in youth sports is parents having issues with other team parents. I have lost a few heartbroken players whose parents forced them to leave their team of friends because they couldn't get along with another parent on the team. Now, make no mistake: if there are parents on a team who are hurting your child's experience, then you should consider changing teams. However, if your child is perfectly content and you make them move against their wishes, then that's all about you.

Another all-time favorite: parents who undermine the coach by questioning their decisions in front of their kids. If you picked the coach, how can you be so critical? If the coach is bad, then you are responsible for picking a bad coach. If you did your due diligence when choosing the coach, you should support them. If you undermine or talk badly about the coach in front of your child, then you are sabotaging a significant relationship for your child. First, your child will be unable to trust their coach's decisions, and this will harm progress. Second, your child will become unhappy because you're unhappy. Kids often dislike things their parents dislike. You are undermining the coach and the player-coach relationship by telling your child that the coach knows less than you.

Lastly, parents who criticize players can cause a litany of problems on a team. First, no one should ever voluntarily criticize someone else's child. Parents vehemently dislike it, and it can devastate the child. Imagine listening to another adult sit and talk about how slow your son is or how badly your daughter is playing. It can cause serious issues.

I once had a player's father tell my nine-year-old goalie that we lost because she missed a save. Outrageous! I had an immediate meeting at the field. The goalie didn't want to say who said it, but I told every parent and player there that if I ever heard of a parent doing that again, the culprit and their child would be asked to leave the team. Zero tolerance is the only policy for this type of behavior.

This can become a team issue because kids talk a lot. If kids hear another player's parents badmouthing them, the relationship becomes strained immediately. If your child finds out, they will be embarrassed. Parents should never share negative opinions about players or coaches with anyone, but especially not with the kids. Anyone who shouts negative remarks risks their child's well-being and their standing on the team.

Summary

Parents are the ones who make youth sports possible. Your role is crucial. You are your children's protector. You need to set the right tone for them and stay consistent. Avoid all the issues listed above and protect your child, even from your own words. Sports can be a great adventure for your family. Make sure you don't turn it into a reflection of yourself or your ego. And always remember that every time your team scores, the other team concedes. They are all kids out there, and we are all responsible for each one of them. Be the adult you want your child to become.

Final
Thoughts

Youth sports can be either a minefield or a sweet blessing for your family. Most parents don't walk into a gym or onto a field intending to lose their temper or get into an argument with rival fans. No sane adult wakes up in the morning thinking, *"Today is the day I embarrass myself at my son's basketball game."* Yet many walk into highly emotional situations completely unprepared for what those moments can stir up. One moment, they are enjoying a cheerful kids' soccer game, and the next, they are a furious "Mama Bear" because someone knocked over their little boy. It's astonishing how quickly our protective instincts can take over—faster and more intensely than most parents expect—especially without preparation, self-awareness, or perspective.

Part of the problem is the culture we absorb from professional sports. For all the excitement they offer, the pro leagues have shaped far too many expectations in youth settings. Professional sports revolve around money—billionaire owners lounging in taxpayer-funded stadiums, players risking everything on the field, and fans paying eighteen dollars for what should be a fifty-cent hot dog. Safety, sportsmanship, and fan behavior only seem to matter when they threaten profit margins. For many young parents, professional sports are the only model they've seen. But that is not the model we want influencing our children's experiences. Youth sports should not echo the aggression, entitlement, or financial obsession of professional sports. They should be something gentler, cleaner, and more meaningful.

Yet parents often enter youth sports full of hope that their child will be the next Alexander Ovechkin, Serena Williams, or Big Papi. Hope is not the issue—dreaming with your child is one of the joys of parenting. The trouble begins when parents confuse dreams with entitlement or believe that the more they invest—more lessons, more elite teams, more pressure—the more greatness will appear. And when it doesn't, some look for someone to blame: coaches, referees, other kids, even their own child.

The truth is simple: if your child is exceptional at something they love, they will still need you—but they will need your support, not your control. They will need your boundaries, not your pressure. They will need your guidance, not your demands. Exceptional talent is rare; expecting it is unrealistic. Preparing yourself, grounding your expectations, and embracing the true purpose of youth sports—that is where every parent can succeed.

If you keep a balanced tone and stay grounded, youth sports can become one of the happiest, healthiest parts of your family's story. If you lose your balance, it can sour the entire experience, no matter how much your child loves to play. I've seen it many times: the kids are often the ones who understand what youth sports are supposed to be, it's the adults who often need reminders.

When I look back on my coaching career through the lens of priorities that matter, I know it has been a success. The responsibility was heavy, yes, but the joy was even greater. I made mistakes—plenty of them—but I kept learning, kept improving, and kept showing up. Most importantly, I built relationships with families and young athletes that continue to mean something to me. Youth sports have given me more than I could ever repay, and thankfully, repayment isn't required. The rewards are the kind that stay in your heart, not your bank account. My hope is that you and your family experience the same growth, joy, and connection.

This book is for *parents who are prepared to make a change.* The ones who show up striving to grow and learn, for their child's sake. That kind of dedication, that willingness to self-reflect and adapt, is what can truly make a difference for the kids. In my opinion, sports parents are some of the finest parents out there. We all know the costs involved—time, energy, emotion, and yes, money—but sports parents willingly shoulder those responsibilities for their children. That willingness to invest, not only financially, but emotionally and holistically, is honorable. It speaks to a depth of care that deserves recognition. Being a parent is hard, and being a sports parent adds to the challenges, but it is all worth it. That is why youth sports must be protected.

I believe deeply in the power of words to inspire better behavior. Two quotes in particular have guided me, and while their origins have been debated, both have stood the test of time.

Edmund Burke's famous words, often dated around 1770, read:

Petronio Morillo

>*The only thing necessary for the triumph
of evil is that good men do nothing.*

John Stuart Mill expressed a similar sentiment way back in 1867:

>*Bad men need nothing more to compass
their ends, than that good men should
look on and do nothing.*

Regardless of who said it better, the message is clear: good people cannot afford to be silent. When caring parents step back, the harmful behaviors win. When good adults remain passive, louder and more destructive voices take over. That cannot continue.

Change in youth sports—and in ourselves—begins with honest reflection. Adults often have a remarkable ability to complicate things that should be simple, even something as pure as a kid's game. That's why the words of Burke and Mill resonate so powerfully: they remind us that good people cannot stay silent or passive. We must stay aware, stay involved, and choose to act when it matters. By reading this book, by opening yourself to new ideas and perspectives, you've already taken an important step. Awareness gives you an advantage now. You can reassess your investment, expectations, and priorities to align with what your young athlete truly needs. It is never too early—or too late—to choose better.

But improving ourselves is only part of the mission. We must also improve the environments our kids grow up in. That means stepping in when necessary. That means speaking up when a parent crosses a line, when a coach behaves inappropriately, or when a child is in distress. A friend once told me about a game in which a mother and her child were being disrespectfully berated while adults stood by doing nothing. That cannot be the standard. We must stand up, and we must stand together.

If you see a parent spiraling, hand them this book. If you see a child hurting, give them a copy and encourage them to share it with their family. One voice can start a conversation. A group of voices can spark a movement. The problems facing youth sports are real and urgent. But the opportunity for change is equally real—and it is in your hands.

And that change begins with you.

Acknowledgments

I want to express my deepest gratitude to my family and friends, who have always supported me. You are my life, and I am genuinely grateful for each of you.

To my family—thank you for your constant love and encouragement. To my sisters, Jennie and Joy, your strength and laughter have meant the world to me. And to my son, Alexander, you are my greatest joy and inspiration. None of this would have been possible without my parents. Thank you, Dad. You made this possible, and you live on in my heart. Thanks to my mom, a talented artist whose spirit and creativity inspire me.

To all my dear friends who stood by me through the difficult times—thank you. Reggie Mason, Steve Hadeed, Johanna Gelber, Rudy Crutchfield, Mark Lucia, Chris Metellus, Vance Rego, Andres Serafini, Dave Ghahhari, Jeff Shirazi, Meredith Mertens, Ryan Mertens, Brittany Mason, Lexy McCarty-Tarrant, Ricky Chappotin, Keith Duley, Rene Sanmartin, Chris Elliott, and finally, Jack and Lucy—thank you for sticking with me.

I am deeply appreciative of my contributors to this work: Rene Sanmartin, Chris Metellus, Evans Malyi, Pete Summerfield, Caroline Kamaris, Richard Gelber, Khuluma Zulu, and my spirit buddy, Rayne Wissman. Your input and collaboration were invaluable. My heartfelt thanks also go to Kay, Jean, and my friend, David—a special appreciation to Johanna, Steve, Betty, and Donnie for your unwavering encouragement.

To all the coaches who educated and guided me along the way—thank you:

› Rene Sanmartin, Director of Youth Programs – Potomac Soccer Association,
› Evans Malyi, Director of Operations – Loudon Soccer Club,
› Chris Metellus, Coach – Liverpool International Maryland
› Johanna Gelber, National Director – Soccer Bugs Child Development Program,
› Alan Kelley, Founder – Alan Kelley Soccer Programs,
› Steve Knapman, Founder – Brit-Am Soccer Academy,
› Rob Ryerson, Head Coach – Howard County Community College,
› Ivan Sampson, Founder – Sampson Soccer,
› Danielle LaRoache, Director of Athletics – The Brearley School,

As well as Pete "Gorgeous" Summerfield, Khuluma Zulu, Luis Rodriguez, Phillip Guay, and Big Willy Kabwasa, your mentorship profoundly shaped me.

Thanks to Christine Keleny at CKBooks Publishing for all the knowledge and support.

Special thanks to Sangita Chari for the foreword and for all your guidance. Your unwavering support took this project to the next level.

Lastly, thank you to every player I have ever coached and to every manager and parent who supported our teams—special shout-out to the Crider, Hirsh, and Libutti families.

I wish you all the very best on your journeys.

With respect, admiration,
and love,
Petronio Morillo

About the Author

Petronio Morillo has spent more than three decades helping young athletes grow on and off the field. A lifelong coach and sports complex manager, he's seen firsthand how powerful—and sometimes challenging—the youth sports experience can be for families. Born in Maryland in 1971, Petronio graduated from American University in 1996 and has dedicated his career to teaching, mentoring, and developing programs that put kids first.

In 2010, he launched a sports-based child development program that now operates in four eastern states and has positively impacted tens of thousands of children. He also coached for Maryland's Olympic Development Program in 2015–2016, further deepening his perspective on the pressures and potential of competitive youth sports. His work is grounded in the belief that sports are more than just games—they're opportunities to teach respect, resilience, and teamwork.

Through his writing and coaching, Petronio helps parents understand how emotional youth sports can be for them—and how their sideline behavior, when unchecked, can unintentionally harm their children's experience. With a helpful and understanding voice, he guides families toward becoming positive, supportive influences in their children's athletic journeys.

∾

If you enjoyed this book and thought it was helpful, please leave a review on your favorite book website and recommend it to anyone you think might benefit from reading it.

~ Thank you